ENVIRONMENTAL EDUCATION

A MANUAL FOR
ELEMENTARY EDUCATORS

ENVIRONMENTAL EDUCATION

A MANUAL FOR ELEMENTARY EDUCATORS

Barbara Robinson
Evelyn Wolfson

TEACHERS COLLEGE, COLUMBIA UNIVERSITY
New York and London 1982

Published by Teachers College Press, 1234 Amsterdam Avenue, New York, N.Y. 10027

First edition published as *Environmental Education Manual* by Elbanobscot, Inc., Sudbury, Mass.

Library of Congress Cataloging in Publication Data

Robinson, Barbara, 1932–
    Environmental education.

    Originally published: Environmental education manual.
    Includes bibliographical references and index.
    1. Human ecology—Study and teaching (Elementary)
2. Nature study. I. Wolfson, Evelyn. II. Title.
III. Title: Environmental education manual.
GF26.R6   1982   372.3'57   82-741
                                          AACR2

ISBN 0-8077-2715-6

Manufactured in the United States of America
87 86 85 84 83 82   1 2 3 4 5 6

Contents

Illustrations

Preface

THE CHALLENGE

In the decade of the 1960s, the United States slowly came to the realization that the Earth's resources are limited and that people's actions are the cause of a rapidly deteriorating environment. By 1970 mounting concern resulted in the proclamation of Earth Week, with its accent on political action, and the passage of the federal Environmental Education Act, which recognized the primary role education must play in bringing about environmental understanding and responsibility.

At that time there was a flurry of activity that brought about new legislation, publications, and organizations. When the rhetoric faded, the continuing challenge to improve the quality of the environment remained for those willing to accept the long-term involvement and commitment entailed in changing the behavior and values of society.

RESPONSE

Until 1979, Elbanobscot, Inc., a nonprofit environmental education center in Sudbury, Massachusetts, met the challenge as a pioneer in environmental education, training teachers and students from all over New England. Its facilities and land holdings were sold to the United States Fish and Wildlife Service in 1979. One innovative program the center had initiated was a pilot environmental aide training course first offered in 1970, which met with enthusiasm. Through community contacts, the center became aware of the growing need for trained aides to assist in teaching and preparing environmental education programs. The training course sought to meet this need.

GROWTH OF THE PROGRAM

The course was offered twice a year from 1970 to 1979. Initially it was open to any interested volunteers with a willingness to learn, concern for the environment, love of the outdoors, and free time for working with schools and organizations. No natural history or teaching background was necessary, although either could be an asset. When it became obvious that many teachers, paid teacher aides, and youth leaders were looking for similar training, the course was offered at an alternate time to enable them to attend. It was also brought to school and youth group locations. Before Elbanosbscot closed its doors in 1979, over 300 participants had taken the course, representing 45 communities and school systems.

DEVELOPMENT OF A MANUAL

As the training course progressed, written materials were put in looseleaf form and distributed to course participants. From 1974 to 1979 a formal manual evolved, which included factual information on ecology and the environment, activities designed to aid course participants in learning and teaching environmental education, bibliographies coded by age level, and, finally, directions for organizing and setting up an environmental education training program.

APPROACH OF THIS MANUAL

This manual is an up-dated and revised version of the original. Although it is organized for participants in an environmental education training course, including teachers, volunteers, and older students, it is also addressed to many different groups seeking better environmental awareness and understanding through direct participation in environmental experiences.

Educators concerned with ways to incorporate environmental education into the curriculum will benefit from the concepts, strategies, and ideas for curriculum enrichment contained throughout this manual.

Teachers, camp leaders, and lay people, interested in an activity sourcebook, will find activities itemized by subject in the index. Additional activity guides and curriculum materials are listed in Appendix B.

Administrators and activists who want to organize an environmental education training program for teachers, students, or volunteers will get helpful information and guidelines, including a course summary in the Introduction and procedures for organizing and evaluating a course in Appendix D.

This manual is not intended to produce specialists in natural history or environmental issues. The main emphasis is on basic environmental education concepts and attitudes and on outdoor activities that can be adapted for all ages and teaching situations. The challenge to become environmentally educated belongs to all levels of our educational system: family, schools, senior citizens' centers, youth groups, and civic clubs alike.

ENVIRONMENTAL ATTITUDES

Environmental problems such as urban decay and contamination of the air and water affect everyone. Yet many do not see a relationship between personal styles of life and the unhealthy environment around them. The problems seem so great and people feel small and powerless. Where to begin?

We believe there are no simple answers to the environmental crisis the world faces today, but that every one of us is part of the problem and part of the solution. If we are to understand how we fit into the environmental picture and how we can respond to environmental problems in a constructive way, we must become aware, informed, and skilled in recognizing and solving problems. In short, we need to become "environmentally educated."

We feel that this education can best come about by direct participation—learning within the environment as well as about the environment. Starting with the immediate—the environment of the home, the school, and the community—we can begin to understand how changes and interrelationships occur and how actions bring about consequences. We can learn how natural systems work and how our human systems are vitally connected.

This environmental education manual spells out this approach in a systematic way.

Acknowledgments

The authors are indebted to these former Elbanobscot staff members: Syma for illustrations; Arlene Nichols and Mary McClintock for reviewing the content and making invaluable suggestions; Kathy Newman for editing, reference, and index contributions; and Jay Craver, Kate Tauesch, Ginny Steel, Becky Ritchie, and other staff personnel for their ideas and assistance. We are also grateful to the many environmental aides who tested and submitted ideas for activities during course sessions. Original revision of this manual was made possible by a grant from the Frances R. Dewing Foundation.

Introduction

There are nine chapters in this manual; each represents a session in the environmental education training course. The first eight chapters provide basic information, activities, and teaching tips on environmental education topics, and the ninth contains course evaluation procedures. References are at the end of each chapter and are separated by level. Appendixes A, B, and C supply supplemental reference information and a source directory. Appendix D provides a set of guidelines for organizing a training course.

For those who wish to peruse this manual and select information and ideas as needed, the table of contents and index will be handy guides. For those who wish to use this manual as part of a formal or informal training course, the following summary of the course with suggested homework for each session will serve as a course syllabus.

COURSE SUMMARY

Session 1. Orientation to Environmental Education Training

Session 1 includes introductions and registration (Figure 1–1), goals of the course, basic environmental education definitions, guidelines for environmental aides, and beginning sensory awareness activities.

Homework   Make an environmental experiences inventory during the week. Look for seasonal signs using all the senses. (See all senses activity in Chapter 1.)

Session 2. Basic Ecology

General ecological concepts are presented in session 2 to help explain plant and animal interrelationships and energy transfer between the physical environment and the living environment. Activities are suggested that reinforce these concepts. The class plays a game, similar to web of life in Chapter 7, to encourage students to make ecological connections. Techniques of observation and inquiry are emphasized in a field activity in which the class must look for examples of change, adaptation, and interaction within a habitat.

Homework   Do a habitat study using field notes.

Session 3. Site Evaluation

Session 3 provides experience on how to inventory a site. It provides a teacher or volunteer a basis on which to start a school program. The session includes ways to make simple maps or plans of a site and a discussion of how to use school grounds for outdoor environmental programs once the grounds have been inventoried.

The class visits either a school site or an open area to determine what is there and how it can be used for teaching purposes. The class can be divided into small groups to cover the following categories: (1) trees, (2) shrubs, (3) ground plants, (4) animals, (5) water and wetlands, (6) landforms, and (7) human-made features. Each group determines variety and types, teaching potential, and limitations or hazards for its category. After a brief period of inventorying, the class shares information and ideas.

Site improvement is also considered, including several types of nature trails. There is training in covering a trail to select teaching stations and to devise study suggestions for each station.

Homework   Visit a school site or selected area to do a general inventory of the flora, fauna, natural, and man-made features. Prepare a simple sketch or map of grounds, using Figure 3–1 (see Chapter 3).

Session 4. Teaching Environmental Education

In session 4 information is given on environmental education concepts and teaching approaches and how they vary for different age levels. The field experience involves observing and evaluating: (1) students outdoors, (2) methods of teaching outdoors, and (3) activities suitable for teaching students outdoors.

This session takes place at a nearby school, nature center, or camp where ongoing programs can be observed. Three different age groups are observed at three successive intervals. During each interval participants observe teachers with environmental education training working with small groups of students.

As a follow-up of this session, additional opportunities are provided for practice teaching. Participants can develop their own activities or use the outdoor activities presented in Chapter 4. For those not yet ready to work alone, a shared assignment or additional observation may be planned.

Homework   Write up an activity that could extend a basic school subject(s) to the outdoors. Be prepared to carry out this activity with a group of children and to evaluate what methods and ideas worked best.

Session 5. Field Trips Workshop

Information is given on how field trips are planned and carried out, and a demonstration field trip takes place. Attention is paid to additional organizational procedures needed for the longer trip, as well as teaching tips on ways to handle potential problems. Suggestions are given for many possible locations for field trip experiences in the community and beyond. Chapter 5 presents a sampling of field trip activities that seem suitable for any part of the country.

Homework   Take a group out on a field trip (see Chapter 5) and report on procedure, theme, and reactions. (Group need not be in a school setting.)

Session 6. Nature and Ecology Workshops

The object of nature and ecology workshops is to make you more comfortable with the physical and living outdoor environment, without feeling the need to know and to be able to identify everything. Brief background material is provided that emphasizes basic characteristics of the subject and simple teaching approaches. The accent is on outdoor activities and related classroom studies that emphasize ecological concepts concerning natural systems.

PLANT LIFE   Plants are the primary producers of the living environment. All other forms of life depend either directly or indirectly on green plants. Trees are one of the more conspicuous green plants and present themselves for easy study. Basic identifying features and simple approaches for the use of keys are given for deciduous and conifer trees.

Homework   Make up your own key using any objects you prefer. (See Chapter 6.)

ANIMAL LIFE   All animals are consumers in the living environment. They can be consumers of green plants, of other animals, or of green plants and other animals. Two major groups in the animal kingdom, Chordata and Arthropoda, are included for study, along with details on several classes within each group. Field activities stress the relationship of animals to each other and to the environment.

Homework   Plan a lesson that will show how an animal meets its basic needs within its habitat (see Chapter 6). Be sure to consider all seasons.

WATER LIFE   Background is presented on water life at various levels of a pond or lake, and activities are included to explore ecological concepts in a water environment.

Homework   Take a group of children to do a water life study using simple equipment discussed in Chapter 6.

PHYSICAL ENVIRONMENT   The effects of weathering, glaciation, and human intervention are explored in an attempt to view the physical environment in terms of how living things, particularly humans, relate to it. Activities include reading the landscape, observing the effects of seasonal change, and exploring energy sources.

Homework   Develop a field activity that relates to the physical environment and uses simple equipment (e.g., sun dial, solar heater, weather vane, compass). See Chapter 6 for suggestions.

Session 7. Enrichment Ideas Workshop

Session 7 discusses games, crafts, and activities with environmental themes for use in an urban setting, on rainy days, to supplement ongoing outdoor education programs, or to provide a change of pace and alternate learning experience within any discipline.

Homework   Design a craft or make up a game for a particular age level, and try it out. See Chapter 7 for suggestions.

Session 8. Environmental Issues

Session 8 explores the community environmental issues and possibilities for environmental action. Educational approaches to the study of community issues include problem solving, role playing, and values clarification. The class is involved in looking at a local issue from many points of view.

Homework Write up a community environmental profile (see Figure 8–1, Chapter 8) during the week. Include information on local environmental problems and programs. Be involved (or involve your class) in one item of specific action in relation to a community problem and report on it.

Session 9. Evaluation and Summary

Evaluation forms (see Figure 9–1, Chapter 9) handed out at the previous session are returned. These give the class an opportunity to evaluate the course content and to state whether personal expectations have been met.

During the final session a review of the goals of the course and of basic ecological concepts lead to group activities that help to evaluate and summarize course content and teaching approaches. The groups are to answer questions or illustrate examples through role playing, problem solving, or other types of presentation to the rest of the class. Unanswered questions and follow-up needs of class members are explored at the end of the session.

ENVIRONMENTAL EDUCATION
A MANUAL FOR
ELEMENTARY EDUCATORS

1 · Orientation to Environmental Education Training

To live at one with the earth,
on a global basis,
will be far and away the greatest challenge
ever faced by man.
If he faces it.
And that is what Environmental Education
is all about.

R. Thomas Tanner
Ecology, Environment and Education[1]

You are invited to participate in a training course that can help you learn more about environmental education and how you can teach others. As a participant, you are asked to fill out the registration form that follows (Figure 1–1) so that sessions can be geared to the needs and interests of those in the training course. Sharing your expectations of the training course will be the first step in your continual participation, and help ensure that class expectations are realistically reflected in the goals of this course.

ENVIRONMENTAL EDUCATION GOALS

The primary goals of the course are: (a) to provide environmental education knowledge, skills, techniques, and practical teaching experience, and (b) to encourage positive attitudes, self-confidence, and motivation to promote environmental education in the home, school, and community.

---

[1]Lincoln, Nebr.: Professional Educators Publications, 1974, p. 97. Reprinted by permission.

Figure 1–1.   Orientation to Environmental Education Training Registration form

Name:_____ Phone:_____

Address:_____

1. List environment-related organizations to which you be-
    long, and indicate any special responsibility (e.g., con-
    servation officer of garden club).
2. List any experience working with students. (This can
    include teaching Sunday School, formal school, special
    tutoring, or working in youth-related organizations such
    as Campfire, Scouts.)
3. State training, business, and professional positions held
    and present occupation.
4. State educational background and any special environ-
    ment courses taken.
5. Indicate any environment-related activities, sports, hob-
    bies that you enjoy.
6. Please explain what you hope to get out of the course.

ENVIRONMENTAL EDUCATION DEFINITIONS AND EXPLANATIONS

What Is Environment?

Each individual relates to and is part of many environments, including the biophysical, cultural, personal, and global or total.

BIOPHYSICAL Biological (living) and physical (non-living) factors

CULTURAL Social, political, economic, scientific, and technological factors; man-made conditions, human institutions, and human interrelationships

PERSONAL Individual interactions and interrelationships in daily life

GLOBAL OR TOTAL The sum of all the above influences and interactions; the concept "Spaceship Earth" as a limited, finite life-support system that we affect and that affects us

The *American Heritage Dictionary* defines *environment* as follows:

The total of circumstances surrounding an organism or group of organisms, specifically: (a) The combination of external or extrinsic physical conditions that affect and influence the growth and development of organisms. (b) The complex of social and cultural conditions affecting the nature of an individual or community.[2]

Noel McInnis expands this definition:

An environment is not a static collection of objects "out there." Rather it is an infinitely great number of factors with which the individual is in constant interaction. . . .

There is no such thing as *the* environment. Environments are plural. There are as many different environments, for humans, as there are human individuals and places that human individuals go. . . .

Environment is anything which is influencing, or being influenced by, something else.[3]

What Is Environmental Education?

Basic characteristics of good environmental education are outlined in the Environmental Education Act (PL 91-516), 1970. They include:

An interdisciplinary approach, emphasizing nature–human interrelationships
A focus on environmental (artificially created and natural) problems relating to the community
Incorporation of informal as well as formal education programs and resources outside the classroom
Development of conservation ethic as well as information
Involvement of all ages
A participant-centered design that allows involvement in the choice of issues and the problem-solving solutions

The following four descriptions of environmental education, along with the above list, provide a comprehensive definition.

Environmental education is aimed at producing citizens (1) knowledgeable concerning their bio-physical environment and its associated problems; (2) aware of how to help solve these problems; and (3) motivated to work toward their solution.[4]

---

[2]*American Heritage Dictionary of the English Language.* 1st ed. s.v. "environment."
[3]Noel McInnis, *You Are an Environment* (Evanston, Ill.: The Center for Curriculum Design, 1972), pp. 41, 46, 48.
[4]William B. Stapp, "The Concept of Environmental Education." *Journal of Environmental Education* 1, no. 1 (1969): 31. Reprinted by permission of Heldref Publications.

Environmental education is an integrated process which deals with man's interrelationships between his natural and man-made surroundings. It is intended to promote among citizens the awareness and understanding of the environment, our relation to it, and the concern and responsible action necessary to assure our survival and to improve the quality of life. It can occur as both formal and informal education.[5]

Environmental education has two major components. . . . One component is termed process education. It is education in the way one learns regardless of subject matter. This component . . . uses the learner's environment to instruct him. . . . The second component is the study of man–environment inter-relationships. This is the content component. Both components are inter-locking and inseparable in a good program of environmental education.[6]

Environmental education is not just something to be taught and learned. . . . [It] is a way of teaching and learning.
Environmental education provides alternate ways of thinking—a synthesis—which colors and affects the humanities, languages, social sciences, history, economics, and religion as dramatically as it does the natural sciences. It will give an ecological perspective for every aspect of learning.[7]

Forerunners to Environmental Education

Nature study, conservation education, outdoor education, and ecology are forerunners of environmental education in the general environmental movement. They all have contributed to basic understandings of the environment in specific ways. None of these older movements received a wide audience in the past because people were not in the center of them, and the survival of the environment and of people was not in question. Today, aspects of these earlier educational approaches are being integrated into a broader approach that emphasizes learning within the environment as well as knowledge about the environment.

Nature study encouraged compartmentalization and a study of specific aspects of natural history, such as ferns or terns, which could be observed in nature or researched in detail at the nature museums that began to spring up.

A concern for *conservation education* emerged out of nature study groups to encourage wise use of our natural resources. The

---

[5]Charles J. Griffith, Edward Landin, and Karen Jostad, *EP—The New Conservation.* (Arlington, Va.: Izaak Walton League of America, 1971), pp. 9–10. Reprinted by permission.
[6]Miriam Dickey and Charles E. Roth, *Beyond the Classroom* (Lincoln, Mass.: Massachusetts Audubon Society, 1971), p. 2. Reprinted by permission.
[7]McInnis, *You Are an Environment,* pp. 29, 44.

term became associated with federal resource programs for better farm and forestry management in the West and with conservation projects by youth groups in the East. It never received the acceptance that was originally sought within the schools.

Outdoor education is still being used to describe studies beyond the classroom and is not limited to nature study. It includes all areas of education that are best taught outdoors. Unfortunately, it has become stereotyped as a camping experience with recreational overtones, such as a week in the White Mountains for the sixth grade.

Ecology has also suffered from being interpreted too narrowly in the past. Since humans are the primary organisms with the ability to control the environment, it is wise that this science now emphasizes, instead of excludes, humans in the study of living things and their interrelationship within the environment.

Why Is Environmental Education Basic Education?

The quality of the environment on Earth has deteriorated to the point that the continued existence of life is threatened. In order to reverse present destructive trends caused by people-related activities and styles of life, an environmental literacy and an environmental ethic must become a basic objective of education at all levels—within school systems, the community, and the home.

Environmental literacy addresses the need to learn how people can live in harmony with the environment. This learning involves understanding natural systems and how human systems relate to them and acquiring basic skills that prepare people to deal effectively with environmental problems and issues.

Environmental ethic is a human value system that promotes the survival of the ecosystem (human and natural). It involves the development of an ecological conscience and responsible commitment. It recognizes that attitudes and values are as important in solving environmental problems as are knowledge and skills.

GUIDELINES FOR ENVIRONMENTAL AIDES

How can trained environmental aides serve schools and community groups in promoting environmental education?

Helping teachers infuse environmental education into existing curricula

Helping students enjoy and learn more from environmental experiences

Helping schools or organizations in collecting, digesting,

preparing, and publicizing information for environmental educational use

Ways Environmental Aides Can Be Used

Teaching assistant: a paid paraprofessional within the school system

Volunteer: works on a regular basis within the school system

After-school volunteer: leads and assists school clubs, youth groups, or community organizations

Resource specialist: receives special assignments on program presentation, field trips, and so forth

Starting Environmental Aide Programs

The initiative for an environmental aide program can come from the principal, a department head, a teacher, a parents' council, the PTA, or an environmental aide. Regardless of the catalyst, the school must support the program. The school must also clearly define job requirements and school rules and protocol.

The work of the environmental aide should be related to the school curriculum. He or she should meet with the principal and teachers before beginning work. The environmental aide needs to feel acceptance and that his or her work is an important contribution.

Guidelines and standards for a volunteer program must be agreed upon at the start. One environmental aide may be sufficient to start a program and to help train additional volunteers. Careful planning at the outset is worth the effort. For a stable volunteer program to be established, a regular schedule needs to be established. Volunteer skills and teacher's needs must also be assessed and related. Someone who is willing and qualified will have to coordinate the work of the volunteers in the school system, and overall professional guidance and supervision are required.

Training and Placement

An environmental aide training program can be organized within a school system or by an environmental group. Recruitment of aides can come through all types of publicity; personal contact with recommended individuals may bring best results.

For each volunteer who indicates a willingness to serve, an assessment of talents, interests, and skills should be made during training. Consultation is helpful during the training phase to assess progress. Records should be kept of progress and activities so that an evaluation of each volunteer can be made at the end of the training. This will help both the schools and the individuals to match specific talents with requests for assistance.

If the program is directed by the schools, a placement coordinator should direct environmental aides to suitable placements.

Avoiding Problems

Certain precautions can be taken to avoid problems with volunteer workers. The volunteer's role must be defined so that dependability and accountability will result. It is essential, although difficult, to give orders and to provide supervision to unpaid volunteers.

If a volunteer uses time in school for personal reasons or discusses confidential information outside of the school, an entire volunteer program can be jeopardized. Be sure the volunteer understands this from the start.

A volunteer, like any employee, may have a personality or other problem that causes friction in the school system. For example, it may be best to avoid using a parent as a volunteer in his or her own child's classes. Such situations may be more difficult to handle than similar ones for the paid worker. Therefore, volunteers need to be placed as carefully as teachers. When relationships do not work out, the aide should be removed or moved to another position. A trial period at the outset would be helpful to see if the aide is suitably placed in terms of abilities and temperament.

Environmental Aide/Teacher Relationship

The teacher is the one in authority and sets the tone for a working relationship. The teacher should indicate the kind of assistance sought and set up a mutually agreeable schedule with the aide. The environmental aide is offering help, not taking over. The aide wants to support, not threaten, the position of the teacher.

The environmental aide can support the teacher by helping with those outdoor experiences that usually require increased adult supervision. The environmental aide can bring to the task certain skills that make additional learning situations possible. This sharing of strengths with the teacher can bring enrichment to the class. The environmental aide can bring background from the community. The aide can help to bridge the gap between the community and the school by promoting better understanding of both, particularly when teachers do not live within the community where they teach.

The teacher can support the aide by providing classroom

preparation and follow-up of the planned environmental activity and by discussing progress of those programs on which the aide is working.

Suggested Qualities for an Environmental Aide

Since the standards for hiring a paid teaching assistant will be determined by the school system involved, we will deal here only with standards for volunteers. For those volunteers who will be associated with schools that do not already have an established volunteer program with clear-cut policies and standards, the following are suggested qualities for environmental aides:

> To have a desire to serve the community in promoting environmental education
> To show professional discretion
> To be sensitive in interpersonal relations
> To be dependable and to adhere to a schedule agreed upon beforehand
> To be flexible and to adapt to the structure of the group with which he or she will be working
> To be cooperative and to use his or her skills to pitch in where needed
> To be a willing learner who is enthusiastic about sharing environmental awareness and outdoor discoveries

Personal Benefits

The personal benefits for environmental aides may include:

> Satisfaction from providing a needed service, that of promoting environmental education, to the community
> Personal growth from meeting a challenge
> Career training in testing personal skills and developing interests, before moving into a professional position
> Enjoyment and learning out-of-doors

SENSORY AWARENESS ACTIVITIES

Young children are naturally curious and sensitive and are eager to become involved in first-hand experiences in the world around them. However, as the learning process advances and children develop cognitive skills, they often lose their sense of wonder and involvement. By the time many are adults, the barriers to receiving information from their senses may be so great that they trust the written or spoken word far more than their own sensory information. Today many adults either intellectualize about environmental problems or feel completely removed from them.

The understanding of environmental concepts and how existing environmental problems can be solved does not come quickly; it is a building process. Out of the many concrete experiences and opportunities to explore and wonder about within a variety of environments comes the understanding of *interrelatedness*. When individuals feel a part of the world around them, they can make a meaningful commitment to protect it.

Environmental literacy includes perceiving with the senses as well as understanding with the mind. A first step in achieving this literacy is to become environmentally aware. A few ideas for awakening the senses of younger children (or reawakening those of older students and adults) are listed below. These are only starting points that can then be expanded upon or modified as you take off on sensory adventures of your own.

SENSE OF TOUCH

FIND YOUR OWN STONE

Purpose   To use touch to get acquainted with a stone and to later identify it.

Equipment   Stones with numbers; blindfolds (optional).

Activity
1. Pass out stones that have numbers written on them.
2. Tell students to become well acquainted with their own stones by feeling them, noting all grooves, bumps, general size, and shape. Tell them to remember the number.
3. Collect stones.
4. Go around circle. Ask student to close eyes (or blindfold) and pick their stone by touch. Check number and return stone.
5. Give a second chance to those needing it, after circle is completed.

Teacher Tips   This can be done in or outdoors. It can also be done outdoors with a tree or, for older students, a "secret place" that they get to know well and must identify later blindfolded.

FEELY BAG

Purpose   To identify objects through sense of touch.

Equipment   Bags containing identical assorted items; blindfolds (optional).

Activity

1. Distribute bags around circle, one for every few students.
2. Ask students to try to identify objects by reaching into the bag (blindfolded or without looking).
3. After all have had a chance to feel, ask students to tell what each thinks is in the bag.
4. Show all items to see if students guessed correctly.

Teacher Tips If done outside and natural materials are used, it can lead to a discussion of where objects come from and what they are used for. Remind students why live things are not used for this activity.

SENSE OF HEARING

MYSTERY BOX **Purpose** To recognize an object by the sound it makes inside a box.

Equipment Box; natural objects.

Activity

1. Place a natural object in box ahead of time.
2. Have each student shake the box to identify object.
3. Compare answers before holding up object.
4. Discuss ways to describe sounds.

Teacher Tips Other objects can be tried out in the same way during the activity, or a different item can be inserted in the box each day. Other ways to guess an item by sound can be tried, such as how it sounds when it is dropped behind a curtain.

STALKING **Purpose** To improve hearing and muscle movements.

Equipment Blindfolds.

Activity

1. Group stands in a circle.
2. Teacher chooses a student to stand in center, blindfolded.
3. Another student is selected by hand signal to stalk student in the center.
4. If center student hears stalker, student points in direction of noise.
5. If stalker tags center student without being caught, they change places.

Teacher Tips A variation of this is predator and prey theme, in which everyone but the predator is blindfolded. Predator has noisemaker and uses it constantly while stalking prey. Blindfolded prey move away from noise within prescribed "safe" area. The first prey tagged changes places with predator.

Sense of Smell

ONION TRAIL **Purpose** To use smell to follow a trail through the woods.

Equipment Large onion.

Activity
1. Rub onion on trees along the trail to mark it (at students' nose levels).
2. Students follow smell to end of marked trail.

Teacher Tips This can be done with garlic, sprigs of mint, or other substances with strong odors. See if some students perceive odors better than others, and discuss perceptual differences.

SMELLS AROUND YOU **Purpose** To use smell to describe an outdoor location.

Activity
1. In defined area students pick a smelling spot.
2. See how many different items can be smelled in their spot. They should vary position—stand, sit, lie, get on hands and knees—and see if different odors are noticed at different levels.
3. See what sharpens sense of smell—holding things close to nose, crushing items in hand (such as leaves), or smelling moist items (such as dirt, stone).
4. Discuss findings in circle.

Teacher Tips Other discussions could include sources of smell; man-made or natural; specific kinds of smell; what smells students like or dislike; the different ways smells are described.

Sense of Sight

COLOR EXPLORATION **Purpose** To look more closely at colors in the natural world.

Equipment Colored tongue depressors or popsicle sticks.

Activity

1. Students are given a colored stick and are to find natural things of the same color in a prescribed area outdoors.
2. Come back together after a few minutes.
3. Everyone goes around to see each other's matching item. Explain that this is better than collecting items.

Teacher Tips   Explanation can follow about what the matching item was doing where it was found. Activity can cover man-made items and can be within classroom or out.

TOOTHPICK HUNT   **Purpose**   To use sight to distinguish colors against natural backgrounds.

Equipment   Toothpicks in various colors.

Activity

1. Toothpicks are scattered in a defined area of field or woods.
2. Students go to defined area and form circle around it.
3. Students scoop up as many toothpicks as are sighted in several minutes.
4. Group comes back together and counts toothpicks collected, sorting into piles by color.
5. Discuss which toothpicks were sighted most often, least often. Why?

Teacher Tips   Follow-up discussion on animal camouflage and adaptation.

SENSE OF TASTE

SPICE CHART   **Purpose**   To identify common spices by taste.

Equipment   Samples of chili powder, cinnamon, cloves, garlic, onion powder, pepper, sage, powdered mustard; paper cups; blindfolds (optional).

Activity

1. Put spices in cups.
2. Blindfold group or have them close eyes and taste spices.
3. After all spices have been tasted, tell students to open eyes and discuss what spices were.
4. Discuss descriptions for spices, including feelings.

Teacher Tips   The cups can be passed around again and students can try to identify same spices by smell. Related activities can be done showing relationship between taste and smell. How do spices (or other foods) taste when holding nose? When not holding nose?

DESCRIBING TASTE

Purpose   To heighten sense of taste.

Equipment   Mint (fruit, peanut, and so forth).

Activity
1. Each student gets a sprig of mint.
2. The mint is chewed and kept in mouth as long as possible while taste descriptions are considered.
3. Students describe what mint was like to taste. How do other senses react?

Teacher Tips   If tasting is used for outside sensory activities, be sure you select a plant you know is edible. Remind students never to taste outdoor things unless they are with an adult who knows!

ALL SENSES

ROLE PLAY ANIMALS IN A SPECIAL HABITAT

Purpose   To use all the senses to imitate how animals live in a field (or some other habitat).

Activity
1. At field (or other habitat) have students sit in circle and have each select an animal that might live or visit there.
2. Students think about and then pretend to be that animal. Ask questions such as what it would see, how it looks for food by smell and sight, how it listens for the enemy, how it gets around.
3. Come back in a circle and discuss what each thinks life is like for selected animal. What senses would be most important?

Teacher Tips   This can be an introduction to a habitat or community study. Older students can consider how the different animals live together in the field and what interrelationships exist. Younger students can guess identity of each other's animals.

ENVIRONMENTAL EXPERIENCES INVENTORY

Purpose   To observe seasonal changes through sensory impressions.

Equipment   Notebook (for older students).

Activity
1. Students go outside for a few minutes each day for a week.
2. Look for signs of the season.

3. Use smell, touch, hearing, taste (with caution), and sight to become aware of the season and how they feel about changes.
4. Record sensory impressions (written, oral, drawing).

Teacher Tips   For older students, the time outside can be longer. The activity can also be done as homework, using classroom to compare student reactions. Seasonal bulletin boards can be made up of student contributions.

A POPCORN PARTY   **Purpose**   To use all senses and have fun!

Equipment   Popcorn, electric popper or stove, skillet, seasoning.

Activity   Self-explanatory.

Teacher Tips   Which sense is used the most in this activity?

REFERENCES

Environmental Education Definitions

ADULTS   Bakshi, Trilochan S., and Zev Naveh, eds. *Environmental Education.* Environmental Science Research Series vol. 18. New York: Plenum, 1980.

Griffith, Charles J., Edward Landin, and Karen Jostad. *EP—The New Conservation.* Arlington, Va.: Izaak Walton League of America, 1971.

McInnis, Noel, and Don Albrecht. *What Makes Education Environmental?* Louisville, Ky.: Data Courier and Environmental Educators, 1975.

Tanner, R. Thomas. *Ecology, Environment and Education.* Lincoln, Neb.: Professional Educators Publications, 1974.

UNESCO-UNEP. *The Belgrade Charter: A Global Framework for Environmental Education.* No. 1, Paris, France: UNESCO, 1976.

U.S. Office of Education, Department of Health, Education and Welfare. "Handbook of Preparing Proposals." *Environmental Education Act* (PL 91–516). Washington, D.C.: Government Printing Office, 1970.

Sensory Awareness

CHILDREN   Scott, John M. *The Senses: Seeing, Hearing, Smelling, Tasting, Touching.* New York: Parents Magazine Press, 1975.

ADULTS   Buell, Larry. *Leader's Guide to the 24 Hour Experience for Environmental Awareness*. Greenfield, Mass.: Environmental Awareness Publications, 1978.

Carson, Rachel. *The Sense of Wonder*. New York: Harper & Row, 1965.

Van Matre, Steve. *Acclimatization*. Martinsville, Ind.: American Camping Association, 1972.

———. 1974. *Acclimatizing*.

———. 1979. *Sunship Earth*.

CURRICULUM GUIDES   Minnesota Mathematics and Science Teaching Project (MINNEMAST) *Using Our Senses*. Minneapolis, Minn.: University of Minnesota, 1971.

———. 1971. *Watching and Wondering*. (K–3)

2 · Basic Ecology

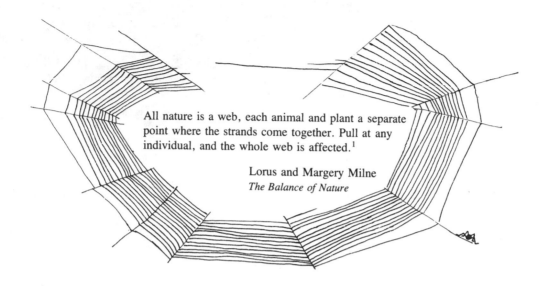

All nature is a web, each animal and plant a separate point where the strands come together. Pull at any individual, and the whole web is affected.[1]

Lorus and Margery Milne
The Balance of Nature

All living plants and animals (including humans) interact in complex ways, and all exchange energy and materials with the physical environment. The study of living things and their relationships to each other and to their physical environment is called *ecology*.

Communities

Ecological relationships are defined by the way organisms function in their environment and how they are affected by other organisms. A *community* is a collection of organisms that live together at a particular time and place. The place in which they live is called their *habitat*. Members of a community have specific needs and are dependent upon one another either directly or indirectly. For example, the robin depends on the earthworm for food as well as on the trees that drop leaves that decay into food for the worms.

Food Webs

Within each community there is a flow of energy from producers to consumers. *Producers* are green plants that trap the sun's energy through a process called *photosynthesis*. *Consumers* are the herbivores that eat the plants; the *carnivores* that eat the *herbivores;* and the *omnivores,* such as humans and raccoons, that eat both the plants and the animals. *Decomposers* are microorganisms that eat waste materials and decaying organisms.

Food Chains

The amount of energy absorbed by a community determines the amount of life the community can support. For example, in a simple field community, the sun's energy is stored in green plants that are eaten by mice, which become food for a hawk. This flow of energy from sun to hawk is referred to as a *food chain*. In a food chain, the producers and consumers store and transfer different amounts of energy. At the primary level, 90 percent of the energy absorbed by plants is lost as heat to the environment. At each additional level, 90 percent of the remaining energy is similarly lost. A food *pyramid* is a graphic representation of this loss of useful energy at each level of a food chain (see Figure 2–1).

Figure 2–1   Sample Food Pyramid

The hawk requires many mice because of energy used in hunting and in maintaining a constant body temperature. The many mice must consume enough green plants to meet their energy needs.

The shorter the food chain, or the more direct the dependence on producers, the less the loss of useable energy. A simple chain is fragile, however, and can be totally disrupted if one species, such as the mice, is no longer available as food. Complex chains with greater diversity provide more balance in a community. Food chains that connect many herbivores, carnivores, and omnivores are called *food webs* because the various needs of the organisms are interrelated and overlapping. Food webs offer stability by providing alternative food sources to less specialized species in a community.

Energy and Matter

Along with the one-way flow of energy in a food chain or web, there coexists a *cycling* of matter. While energy is always being lost as heat, it is balanced by new energy being absorbed through photosynthesis. There is a fixed amount of matter, however, that must be recycled. Forms of matter, such as hydrogen, oxygen, nitrogen, carbon, phosphorous, and sulfur, are most essential to life. Over 30 other elements are important in trace amounts. Elements and compounds are continually recycled from air, water, and soil through food webs and through the work of microorganisms like bacteria, molds, and fungi, which decompose organic materials.

Living things obtain the energy and matter needed to survive by interacting with their physical environment and with each other, within an *ecosystem*. Ecosystems can be as small as a pond or a rotting log or as large as a forest. Major ecosystems, or life zones, are called *biomes,* and the total of all the various ecosystems and their interactions is called the *ecosphere* or *biosphere*.

Manufactured Substances

When synthetic substances enter a food chain they often become concentrated at the upper end of the chain. For example, in the past chlorinated hydrocarbon insecticides were used to kill a variety of insect pests by spraying. The dead insects were eaten by birds, the next member of the food chain. You might think the effects of the pesticide would diminish as each consumer becomes involved. However, the opposite is true. The pesticide is not excreted by the organisms and is very stable. It is passed along and becomes concentrated in the highest member of the food chain because the higher the animal the greater the quantity of the food source consumed.

Ecological Relationships

Each organism in a community is there because the environmental conditions necessary for it to carry on its way of life are provided for in an *ecological niche*. Each organism has a place or niche based upon what it does. For example, deer and red fox are both members of the deciduous forest. Deer live around clearings near water where they browse on twigs and leaves. In the clearings they look for certain weeds. They will eat nuts, water lilies, and acorns. Red fox also like a woodland area with mixed cover. Their diet consists mostly of mice, then fruits and vegetables. Thus, these two forest animals occupy different niches within the same habitat.

Adaptation

If conditions are not favorable for a plant or animal, it must change or *adapt* to suit its environment. If it cannot adapt, it will not survive. A given set of climatic and physical factors will support a specific type of plant and animal life. Each time the factors are changed, a predictable series of changes will take place until a new stability is achieved. For example, New England was once covered with a mixed hardwood–hemlock forest. The settlers cleared the land for farming. When the fields were abandoned, juniper and cedar appeared, then pine, and finally seedlings of the hardwoods returned to get a start in the shade of the pine. This is known as *succession*.

Succession

Succession causes changes in the amounts and kinds of organisms in a community. A *population* within a community is one species of plants or animals that are living and reproducing together. For example, in the oak forest one of the populations is the oak tree and another is the chipmunk. In the meadow there are many populations of different grasses. All populations are linked together through the food chain, and natural controls work to keep nature in balance. Some of these controls are fire, disease, loss of food, water pollution, and predators. There is an interdependence among plants and animals for food and shelter, and where a community appears stable, it is considered to be a *balance of nature*. When any one population of a community is changed, the balance of nature is altered and all members readjust to reach a new balance. Some members may increase in number and/or some may die out totally in this process.

Human Communities

Human communities also interact with one another. For example, large populations need vast amounts of food, and large farms require man-made fertilizers from industry. Each community is dependent on the other, as shown in Figure 2–2.

Figure 2–2   Human Communities

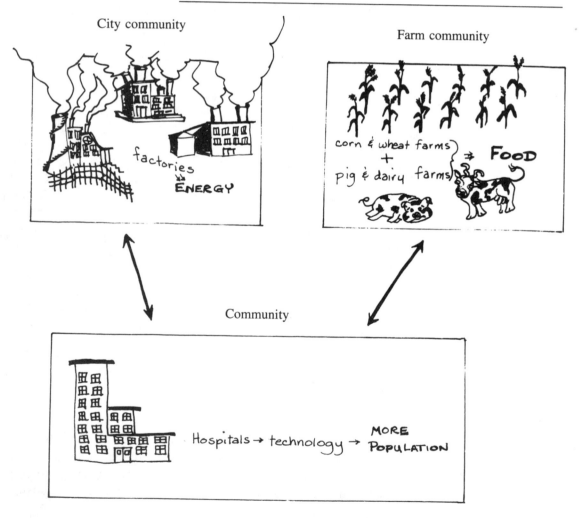

In the past 10 years the study of ecology has increased in importance because the use of technological processes in farming, industry, and mining has affected our air, water, and food chain. Fertilizers are being washed into our waterways producing an abundance of nutrients that accelerate vegetative growth in our waterways, eventually causing them to clog. Industry has been using poisonous chemicals like PCBs (polychlorinated biphyenls) in the manufacture of electrical equipment, plastics, and other products. These industrial pollutants enter our lakes, rivers, and oceans through sewer pipes and are incorporated by lower life forms and ultimately by fish. In addition, people are dependent upon energy resources that are finite: oil shale, coal, petroleum, and natural gas. In the mining and consumption of these resources, we have polluted our land, air, and water.

Since world population is increasing faster than world food productivity and since efforts to increase productivity are causing deleterious effects around the globe, we must learn how to meet our growing needs without permanently damaging our environment and wasting our natural resources.

CONCEPT DEVELOPMENT

The study of ecology should involve students in direct experiences whereby they explore their own environments. Well-planned science curricula include social and environmental problems in scientific learning. Moreover, it is the goal of environmentalists to see that environmental education is integrated into all disciplines, not just science.

The concepts presented throughout a curriculum series from kindergarten to grade six are fairly standard. Some concepts are briefly stated for the nonteacher who may not know the sequence at which various ecological concepts are presented. These concepts can be used in any subject area to relate specific learning skills to the broader picture, that is, the relationship of the learner to the environment. This is merely an aid to help focus outdoor studies on the understanding and skills of specific age groups.

PRIMARY   Colors, shapes, sizes, textures, living versus nonliving, observation skills

LEVEL 1   Living versus nonliving; basic needs of plants and animals, including the child; habitats; change

LEVEL 2   Basic needs of *individual* organisms (including the student)—food and water. Each has own cycle. Compare similarities and differences. Reinforce concept of living versus nonliving

LEVEL 3   Populations (*groups* of organisms, including people). Interaction; interdependence. People as populations interacting with all other populations. People's actions important to natural world

LEVEL 4   Changes in world around us—water, solar energy, time, the atmosphere, the school, home, community as an environment. Natural (including man-made) environments

LEVEL 5   Populations form communities. Interdependence; food chains; food webs; niches; producers and consumers exchanging energy. Changes made by people sometimes slow to show deleterious results

LEVEL 6   Human needs passed down by tradition. Some needs wasteful. Human's manipulation of environment. Individual responsibility; group action; ecosystems

BASIC ECOLOGY ACTIVITIES

TAKING FIELD NOTES
ON A HABITAT

Purpose   To take field notes on a particular habitat over a period of 1 week. To observe and record details on plants, animals, and their interrelationships.

Equipment   Small notebook or drawing paper and pencil. Useful, but not necessary: hand lens, field guides, binoculars, knapsack.

Activity   Take a field trip to a nearby habitat to record daily observations. This activity is designed to be carried out at regular periods for at least 1 week. Remind students to observe differences, similarities, patterns, interactions, and changes within the habitat. Subtle changes will appear that would not be observed at a single viewing. Field notes should include the following:

1. *Date and time*   Record for each field notation.
2. *Field location*   Be short but precise as you may want to return to the same spot another season or direct others to this exact location.
3. *Conditions*   Season, temperature, wind, amount of light, water, and distance from which observations made.
4. *Physical environment*   General description of area, including soil, rocks, slope, vegetative cover, and outstanding natural features.
5. *Organisms*   What kinds of plants and animals live in this community? How do they relate to each other and to the

environment? What are the relative sizes of populations? What kinds of interactions are taking place? A general description of organisms is sufficient (grasses, shrubs, insects), and specific names are not necessary. What possible factors influence their survival here? Consider niche, food chain, food web, adaptation, and other laws of life. If larger animals (including humans) are not present, look for evidence of their activities or speculate about what animals could survive under the prevailing conditions. Remember that insects are available year round for observation, so use a hand lens.

Teacher Tips   This can be used as a homework assignment instead of a group activity. Younger students should be limited to 5 or 10 minutes in the field and can draw pictures of the habitat rather than take notes.

Follow-Up
1. If the habitat study is done as a group, have students compare notes to see how different observations can be made in the same area. Are some student descriptions very visual? Very audio? Very detailed?
2. Have young students draw pictures of the habitat and put them together to form a mural.
3. Visit the same habitat at several different seasons. Compare these notes with those taken at other times of the year. How have things changed?

GENERAL ECOLOGY
ACTIVITIES

Purpose   To introduce a variety of ecological concepts through the use of games, field studies, collecting, and analyzing.

Equipment
Activity 1.   Paper, crayons, cards, and field guides.
Activity 2.   Small plastic bags.
Activity 3.   Small container.
Activity 5.   Small container.
Activity 7.   Waterproof footwear and old clothing.
Activity 8.   Paper and pencil.

Activity
1. *Animal characteristics and needs*   Pin to the back of each student a slip of paper with the name of an animal on it. Each student tries to discover his or her own identity by asking questions about the animal's structure, food, habitat, and so forth that can be answered with a "yes" or "no." (Simple field guides should be available unless students have been studying these animals.) This activity works well when done in pairs.

When players find out their animals' identities, the slips of paper are moved to their fronts.

a. *Animal classification* The game may be expanded by asking the group to divide up according to categories such as insect, bird, reptile, or mammal.

b. *Food chains* Students can arrange themselves according to what the animals eat (vegetable or meat). The web of life and interrelationships can be discussed as students move into the appropriate places.

c. *Habitats* Place large printed cards with habitat names (air, water, forest, field, underground) in different locations. Have the students locate and stand near the habitat in which the animal they represent lives.

2. *Soil* Soil is the principal source of minerals and water needed by plants. It is both living and nonliving. Go outdoors with small baggies and have the students make their own soil. It will be interesting to see what they come up with and will provide a good starting point for other ecological activities.

$\frac{1}{2}$ { Air and water (necessary for organisms to live and work)

+

$\frac{1}{2}$ { Rock particles (minerals come from weathering)
Organic material (living or once-living material)
Recycling organisms (fungus, molds, bacteria, earthworms)

When each person has finished examining the materials in his or her bag, have the contents of the bags returned to the outdoors. This will reinforce the concept of conservation of resources.

3. *Population* Students to choose a tree in spring and collect as many seeds as they can find on the ground under the tree. Count the seeds, and see how many trees would result if all reached maturity. List the animals and plants that keep the population of this tree under control by feeding on it. Older students can total up the results of several generations, should all seeds survive and multiply at the same rate.

4. *Adaptation* Tell students to sit quietly on a mowed field of grass and look closely at the ground. Ask them the following questions: Do you see many small reddish brown ants running around? Would you be able to see them better if they were

purple or yellow? Camouflage through color and pattern is an important adaptation. It protects animals from their predators. Look for other insects in the grass. What color are they? Are they hard to find? What color would you choose to be if you lived in a pine forest on the ground? On the leaves? In the bark?

5. *Change* Take a walk and have each student locate one example of an organism that is undergoing or will undergo change. Collect organisms only if it will do no damage. Otherwise, mark the item by tying a tiny piece of colored yarn around it. Examples:

   a. A seed will become a plant
   b. A flower will become a seed
   c. A caterpillar will become a moth or butterfly
   d. Wood will become soil
   e. Rock will become sand

   Does everything become something else? Think of things that do not change. Man-made products often change so slowly that they appear not to change.

6. *Human Impact on an Ecosystem* Students can choose the ecosystem of an urban, suburban, or rural area. Have them take a walk and list all the signs of human activity that have changed the land, for example, a fence, a road, mowed fields, trash, buildings, telephone poles. Discuss the impact of these items. Where was the fence placed on the landscape? If it is around a field, did it change the field community? How? Small animals might not be able to get through the fence and the make-up of the field community will change. Was the building placed on wet land that had to be filled? If so, that land can no longer act as a sponge and will redirect water. Do not assume human impact is bad. Evaluate the changes. Plowed fields allow different communities to develop. Fields are different but no less desirable than forests. Field communities are also important ecosystems.

7. *Ecosystem* Have students take a walk to a swamp or marsh and pick up a handful of soil. Tell them to smell it, to rub it between their fingers. How does it feel? A swamp is a big wet compost heap. Birds, fish, frogs, and bats eat insects that are born and hatch here. Rabbits and muskrats come to eat the lush grasses. Decaying plants, in addition to becoming food for microscopic animals, are continuously cycling nitrogen, carbon, phosphorous, and other elements into the environment. Have students squeeze their swamp muck. Is there a lot of water in it? A swamp absorbs water during wet seasons and slowly releases it when the surrounding lands dry out. You could call a swamp a big sponge.

The ecosystem of a marsh is the interwoven food relationships between and among the plants and animals of the marsh community together with their physical environment (see Figure 2–3).

Figure 2–3   Ecosystem of a Marsh

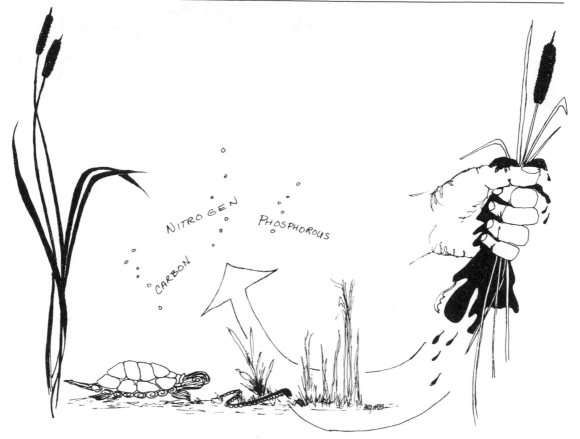

8.   Have each student make a list of his or her intake for the previous day and arrange the items in a food chain or pyramid.

Teacher Tips   Most activities can be conducted with any age group. However, younger children do best with short trips out-of-doors and drawings can replace field notes.

REFERENCES

Ecology

CHILDREN   Alexander, Taylor R., and George S. Fichter. *Ecology*. Golden Guide Series. New York: Golden Press, 1973.
Blough, Glenn O. *Discovering Cycles*. New York: McGraw-Hill, 1978.

Farb, Peter. *The Story of Life: Plants and Animals Through the Ages*. New York: Harvey House, 1962.

————. and the editors of *Life*. *Ecology*. New York: Time–Life, 1963.

Lerner, Carol. *On the Forest Edge*. New York: William Morrow, 1978.

————. 1980. *Seasons of the Tallgrass Prairie*.

Oliver, Jane. *The Living World*. Oklahoma City, Okla.: Warwick, 1977.

Pringle, Lawrence. *Chains, Webs and Pyramids: The Flow of Energy in Nature*. New York: Thomas Y. Crowell, 1975.

ADULTS Blaustein, Elliott, and Rose Blaustein. *Investigating Ecology. A Student-Oriented Project Book for the Detailed Study of Ecology*. New York: Arco, 1978.

Brainerd, John W. *Nature Study for Conservation*. New York: Macmillan, 1971.

Brown, Vinson. *The Amateur Naturalist's Handbook*. Englewood Cliffs, N.J.: Prentice-Hall, 1980.

Buchsbaum, Ralph, and Mildred Buschbaum. *Basic Ecology*. Pittsburgh, Pa.: Boxwood Press, 1957.

Hillcourt, William. *Field Book of Nature Activities and Hobbies*. New York: G.P. Putnam's Sons, 1970.

Milne, Lorus J., and Margery Milne. *Ecology Out of Joint: New Environments and Why they Happen*. New York: Charles Scribner's Sons, 1977.

————. *The Balance of Nature*. New York: Alfred A. Knopf, 1960

Storer, John H. *The Web of Life*. New York: New American Library, 1972.

————. *Man in the Web of Life*. Old Greenwich, Conn.: Devin-Adair, 1980.

3 · Site Evaluation

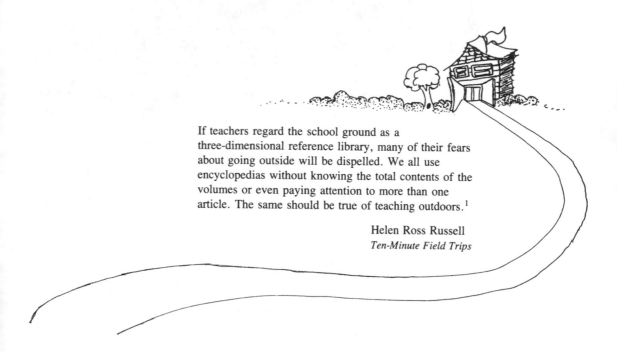

If teachers regard the school ground as a three-dimensional reference library, many of their fears about going outside will be dispelled. We all use encyclopedias without knowing the total contents of the volumes or even paying attention to more than one article. The same should be true of teaching outdoors.[1]

Helen Ross Russell
Ten-Minute Field Trips

USING SCHOOL GROUNDS

School grounds are a good place to start teaching outdoor environmental education. They provide a maximum of opportunity with a minimum of fuss, they are easily accessible and convenient, and no funds, permissions, insurance, or transportation are necessary.

School grounds can be used right away. The natural and man-made environments of the school site can enhance educational opportunities.

School grounds allow the teacher to be spontaneous and to take advantage of the "explorable instant" when the classroom door can be open at the point most relevant to the ongoing study. They allow children the chance for first-hand, varied experiences that make the classroom study more relevant and exciting.

Brief occasions outdoors that prepare students for longer field trips are possible. When the field excursion or camping trip occurs, students will have developed the receptivity, insight, and behavior to make the most of the longer and more unusual experience. Students can develop certain skills that are better learned

[1]Chicago, Ill.: J.G. Ferguson, 1973, p. 4. Reprinted by permission of H.R. Russell.

outdoors, such as using all the senses for awareness and observation, using manual skills, learning to cope, and learning the process of individual inquiry and problem solving.

All school sites can be used for educational purposes, regardless of size and type of group. All sites have soil, plant, and animal life, even if black topped. They are all affected by weather and climate. All sites relate in some way to the community or neighborhood around them.

Past and present interrelationships between human beings and the environment can be studied on all sites.

ANALYZING SCHOOL GROUNDS

Figure 3–1 is a sample of a form used for evaluating school sites. An inventory of the site's features should include outstanding physical and man-made features, and the potential for educational activities. Students can be involved in the development, evaluation, and follow-up of projects. It is important to remember that a schoolyard inventory is a beginning and not an end in itself.

PLANNING AND MAINTENANCE

Student involvement in projects, such as building a log discussion center or a small bridge or developing a nature trail, is not only good education, it is good economics. If students help plan a project and know why it is being undertaken, they will also help to ensure that proper respect for the area will be established and upheld.

Expensive, permanent structures are not wise. Free materials can usually be obtained from parents or the community. For example, logs and wood chips might come from the local tree department or telephone and power companies.

If large projects are undertaken that require more strength and equipment than available through the school (such as building a dam or creating a pond), an approved plan and funding will be necessary. If no funds are available in the budget for these special developments, the parent–teacher group or the children themselves can help earn the money. Consult government conservation groups for free assistance. Parent–teacher groups can also be encouraged to contribute a small amount of money for simple equipment, such as compasses and shovels, and for environmental education training for teachers and volunteers.

If several groups are using a school ground for different projects, it is a good idea to coordinate activities to avoid duplica-

Figure 3–1. School Site Inventory

Name and location of site   Name of reporter
Parking and access   Date of inventory
                                  Approximate acreage

OUTSTANDING PHYSICAL FEATURES (DESCRIBE VARIETY AND TYPES IN GENERAL TERMS)

Plants: Trees
          Shrubs
          Ground plants
Animals:
Water, wetlands:
Geological Features:
Habitats (e.g., woods, fields):
Other:

OUTSTANDING MAN-MADE FEATURES:

Buildings:
Parking areas, roads:
Play areas and equipment:
Maintained areas (such as lawns):
Energy and waste systems (such as power, trash, sewage):
Other:

POTENTIAL FOR EDUCATIONAL ACTIVITIES

To what extent is the site already used for environmental education?

What is the potential for using the site beyond its present use?

What are the limiting factors for teaching outdoors (such as, dangerous conditions, lack of varied habitat, poisonous plants)?

Is there a written inventory or map of site already available?

List persons or offices to contact for additional information on this site.

On a separate piece of paper, prepare a rough sketch of the site, including boundaries, buildings, distinguishing features, and present and potential educational study areas.

tion of effort or conflicting projects at the same location. A central clearinghouse or site coordinating group is helpful to insure cooperative use of inventories, maps, trail booklets, or any other information.

COMMUNITY RELATIONS

Aside from community assistance on planning and development, contact with the community can occur in other ways. Community volunteers, consultants, and environmental aides can provide needed resources to help keep school ground programs functioning. Allowing community use of school grounds for nature study and recreation during nonschool hours helps promote an understanding of the educational aspects of the site and builds support for the concept of outdoor environmental education.

NEW SITE DEVELOPMENT

Planners, conservationists, and educators can all impress upon the architect and school site committee the importance of topography in locating a new building so that the site will not be ruined in terms of its natural environment (see Figure 3–2). Seek community support in encouraging proper use of soils for drainage, preservation of natural features such as hills and wet areas, and setting aside of areas where views or features make feasible outdoor study sites.

Figure 3–2   Site Development Map

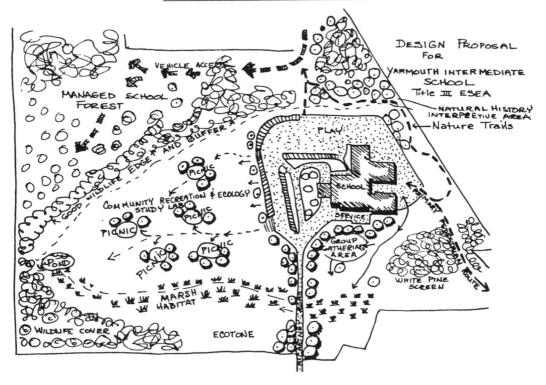

School ground curriculum enrichment can take place outdoors with all subjects. A few examples of how the school site can be used in general ways to augment the existing curriculum include:

Science   Plant studies, including nursery and garden plots; animal life studies; water (properties, life); ecology (such as communities, habitats, ecosystems,); use of scientific inquiry and problem-solving methods

Math   Number concepts, measurement, mapping, estimating, using equipment (such as clinometers, compasses)

Language arts   Using senses for inspiration, listening, and expression; creative writing in natural setting; vocabulary

Social studies   History; map making, geography, landforms; people–land relationships in the past; the school site as an introduction to the larger community

Arts, crafts   Using nature's litter for creative art projects such as collages, mobiles, block prints; understanding colors, forms, patterns in nature; scenes for drawing

Music, games   Can take place in the outdoor environment to provide needed change of pace, fun; rhythms in nature—notes, tones, and timbres

If the site lacks variety or suitable locations for study, development and use projects can make the site more inviting for environmental education activities. Comparative studies of soil, plant, and animal life can be made before and after improvements.

A more varied environment can be created by plantings and by the development of special teaching areas set apart from regular school ground activities such as nursery, weather station, erosion management area, succession plot, herb garden, pond area.

A printed handbook or inventory of a site could become a guide for the school and community, helping others to use the school grounds. Nature trails can be laid out. If a self-guided nature trail is established, a write-up can be included in the handbook or printed separately. Outdoor classroom area(s) can be established.

Outdoor Classroom

The whole school site may be considered an *outdoor classroom,* but usually the term applies to an area designated as an outdoor study site because it lends itself to regular teaching opportunities.

It usually has a varied habitat, a good learning atmosphere, and some privacy from the distractions of playground or road areas. A log arrangement that provides a discussion center is easy to make and is very useful.

More and more uses and benefits can be derived from moving a classroom outdoors. However, the outdoor classroom area should not become a duplication of the school classroom. Having an outdoor classroom does not mean that other areas of the school site cannot be used or that field trips to more distant locations are less desirable. An outdoor classroom area is just one of many ways to use a school site and one of many approaches to learning about and interrelating with the environment.

Teacher Tips

The following suggestions will help ensure that the activities are carried out as safely and enjoyably as possible.

Make sure dangerous hazards are not included in study areas and that children are prepared for any problems that do remain such as poison ivy, bees, poisonous plants, wet areas. Avoid overuse of any one spot where traffic might destroy the plant and animal life. Devise means to rotate paths and to protect paths from erosion.

Make sure school ground boundaries are clarified so that the students do not trespass on private property. If there is an interesting vacant lot or other possible area for study adjacent to the school site, get permission before using.

Older students or community assistants can be used to set up smaller study groups and provide resources on particular topics. A soil conservation service consultant might point out ways to keep erosion to a minimum, and a tree surgeon might show tree rings and explain tree diseases. A parent or retired person can be trained to assist in general environmental experiences.

NATURE TRAIL APPROACHES

Purposes

A nature trail can provide many benefits. It promotes a continuing experience outdoors. It encourages group cooperation in planning and in outdoor skills. It provides a service to others who can also use the trails to enjoy and understand the environment. It can act as a stimulus to learning about environmental interrelationships.

Trail Planning

Determine what kind of trail is needed and how it should be developed. Consider the location, length, and type of trail desired.

Location   Select a location on a school ground or another site that contains varied features and points of interest. It must be away from school ground activity and playing fields. Take into consideration the effect the trail will have on the area, and avoid fragile or dangerous environments.

Length   The basic trail should be not more than one-half mile. On a school site it will probably be much shorter. Any connecting loop (see types of trails) should be long enough to be a separate trail in itself.

Type of Trails   There can be one basic trail, such as an oval, a figure eight, or a winding path with a separate entrance and exit, with one or more connecting loops or spurs as specialty trails. See Figure 3–3 for a sample trail map. The details of the trail will depend upon size and variety of the site, age of group, and amount of outside help available.

Preparation

Know the boundaries of the site on which you will be working so as to avoid trespassing. If your trail is to go outside the school grounds, get permission from owner of grounds. If a school site is to be used, check to see that no other group is undertaking a similar project. (Could you work together?) Check to see if there is a master plan for the school site or a school site committee that you should consult. (This would be true for any site.)

Has an inventory of the area already been done? If so, review it with your students before going out (or refer to it in the field). If not, preparing the inventory can help determine the best location for the trail. Keep a notebook on the project, organization, site evaluation, and other information that may be included later in a self-guiding booklet or in a classroom follow-up activity.

Do not make the project too demanding for the age group. Vary the hard work with fun. As teacher, carry on only where needed. Cooperative efforts by students are part of the educational process of building the trail. If assistance is needed from outside experts or older students, encourage interaction.

Development   Choose an area with varied terrain that is not too steep, rough, or dangerous. Mark the area designated for the trail

Figure 3-3   Elbanobscot Winter Search Map

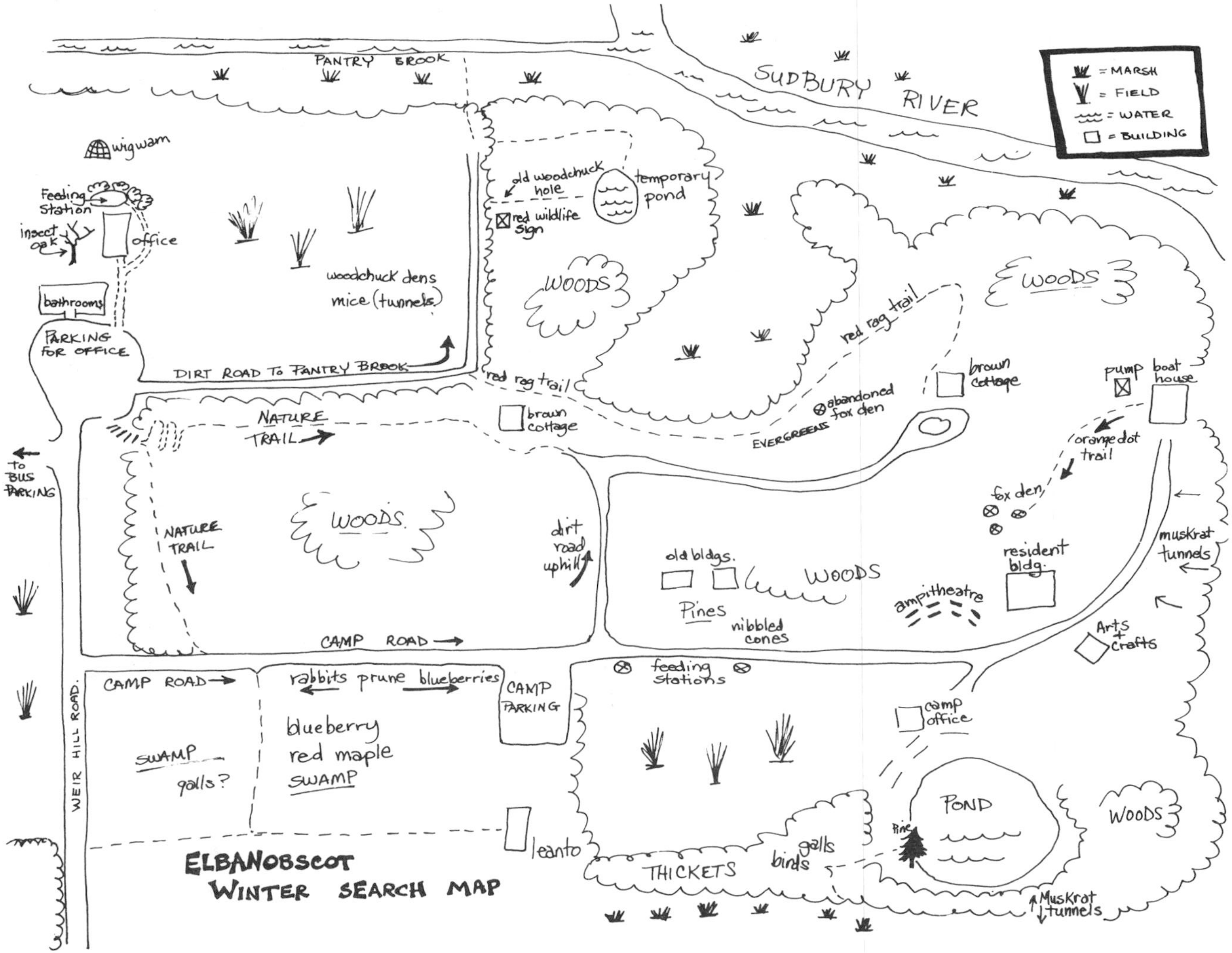

with string, colored tape, or other marker. Avoid large trees and rocks. Prune, cut, and clear a footpath wide enough for single-file use. Leave only ground cover that can withstand human trampling. A narrow, winding path encourages exploration and a sense of remoteness. A path across a slope rather than up and down minimizes erosion. A straight line path can be monotonous. Avoid sharp turns that encourage shortcuts. Provide special stopping places for demonstration and study use, such as an archaeological or geological feature, soil erosion, or succession example. Save some of the brush to use for animal homes in a suitable location for attracting wildlife. Provide loops for special activities such as a sensory walk, a colonial study, or a fern trail.

Equipment   Tools such as pruners, loppers, spades, rakes for pruning, cutting, clearing; tree pruning paint; wooden or plastic markers; tape, stakes, string; saw, axes, picks (for older students or community helpers).

Activity   Cost and vandalism make it necessary for markers to be simple and practical. Experiment to see what weathers best, is most secure, and is most conducive to continual learning approaches. Durable wooden markers with numbers can relate to a map or to a self-guiding booklet. Temporary markers can be used and collected after the trail activity. Interpretive signs are possible. Put markers in the ground to avoid damaging trees.

Follow-Up   Once a basic trail developing activity is accomplished, programs can be undertaken to make the trail more useful. After the first group has cut the trail, other groups may organize their own activities for trail use. The trail should be a schoolwide educational tool rather than a finished product of one group. Mapping, inventorying, and working up interpretive material can be done over and over again. Try to involve as many people of all ages in its development and continuing use. The trail is a beginning tool and not a final product.

NATURE TRAIL CURRICULUM ENRICHMENT

In addition to the general suggestions already made on school site use, nature trail activities can involve:

Industrial arts, shop   Making signs and markers
English   Writing a self-guiding trail booklet; looking up information about flora and fauna; researching study questions; reading, telling, or acting out stories outdoors; writing poems and stories

Physical education   Outdoor exercise and coordination

Science   Inventory of plants and animals; classification and use of keys; weather and climate studies; ecological inter-relationships

Social studies   Previous land use along the trail; geography and mapping; Colonial and Indian use of plants for food, medicine, and so forth

Art   Drawings; visual presentations on trail features; craft projects

REFERENCES

School Grounds

ADULTS   Brainerd, John W. *Nature Study for Conservation*. New York: Macmillan, 1971.

Crisp, Wymlee. *Development and Uses of the Outdoor Classroom: An Annotated Bibliography*. Metuchen, N.J.: Scarecrow Press, 1975.

Educational Facilities Laboratory. *Environmental Education/Facility Resources*. New York, 1972.

————. 1972. *Something More You Can Learn from Your Schoolhouse*.

Gross, Phyllis, and Esther P. Railton. *Teaching Science in an Outdoor Environment*. Berkeley: University of California Press, 1972.

Marsh, Norman. *Outdoor Education on Your School Grounds. Manual for Elementary and Junior High Teachers*. Sacramento, Calif.: Office of Conservation Education, 1968.

Roth, Charles E. "Questions and Answers About Outdoor Classrooms." Mimeographed. Lincoln, Mass.: Massachusetts Audubon Society, 1971.

U.S. Forest Service, Department of Agriculture. "Teaching Conservation Through Outdoor Education Areas." Washington, D.C.: Government Printing Office, 1970.

Nature Trails

ADULTS   Ashbaugh, Byron L., and Raymond Kordish. *Trail Planning and Layout*. New York: National Audubon Society, 1965.

Cooperative Extension Service. "A Guide for Developing Nature Trails." Extension folder No. 66. Durham, N.H.: University of New Hampshire, 1968.

Margolin, Malcolm. *The Earth Manual*. Boston, Mass.: Houghton Mifflin, 1975.

Mohr, Charles E. "How to Build a Nature Trail." Audubon Nature Bulletin, Part of Set NB 2. New York: National Audubon Society, 1953.

Outdoor Biology Instructional Strategies (OBIS). *Trail Module—Trial Edition*. Berkeley, Calif.: Lawrence Hall of Science, 1976.

U.S. Department of Agriculture, Forest Service. "Developing the Self-Guiding Trail in the National Forests." Publication No. 968. Washington, D.C.: Government Printing Office, n.d.

VanderSmissen, Betty, and Oswald H. Goering. *Leader's Guide to Nature-Oriented Activities*. 3rd ed. Ames, Ia. Iowa State University, 1977.

4 · Teaching Environmental Education

A thorough understanding of the teaching and learning processes and the principles of human development is essential for a teacher who desires to engage students in relevant, individualized environmental education. As he selects, plans, and implements such education for his students, he should try to take into account how children learn, so that his established goals can be achieved.[1]

Larry L. Sale and Ernest W. Lee
Environmental Education in the Elementary School

EFFECTIVE GENERAL LEARNING APPROACHES

Students learn best when the following learning approaches are used in education:

Learning by doing—through first-hand learning, hands-on activities, direct experiences inside and outside the classroom

Focusing on what is real and relevant to each student

Learning through discovery, inquiry, and problem solving to develop individual initiative and self-evaluation

Using senses and feelings, as well as the mind

Relating new experiences to a larger picture, or parts to the whole

Building on past experiences to extend and develop concepts and skills

Encouraging positive group interaction that enhances individual self-esteem

---

[1] © 1972 by Holt, Rinehart and Winston, Inc. Reprinted by permission of Holt, Rinehart and Winston, p. 41.

EFFECTIVE LEARNING APPROACHES IN ENVIRONMENTAL EDUCATION

Environmental education can make use of all these learning approaches in the process of producing literate and responsible citizens who are concerned with living in harmony with the environment. When considered as a way of teaching all subjects, rather than as a separate subject to be taught, environmental education has the following special aspects.

Environmental education is a way of looking at things in terms of interrelationships (connections between the individual and the environment; between cause and effect; between changes and consequences) that makes any subject more meaningful and relevant. Since environmental concepts are unifying and are not limited to a particular subject, they can be integrated into existing subjects or can be the focus of interdisciplinary or multidisciplinary studies.

Environmental education emphasizes environmental attitudes as much as factual information. The subject matter is so wide ranging and comprehensive, many consider it too difficult to teach as a separate part of the curriculum. It encourages learning how to learn and uses the world beyond the classroom for this purpose.

FEARS OF TEACHING OUTDOORS

Some fears teachers will need to overcome before involving students in environmental experiences beyond the classroom include:

Fear of the unknown outdoors and preference for the predictable and secure classroom environment

Physical fear of danger outdoors and of creepy, crawly things

Fear of loss of control and discipline problems outside the classroom

Worry about not knowing an answer; lack of confidence about identification of natural objects and features

Fear outdoor experiences will take too long and required curriculum will not be covered

Concern that learning benefits cannot be measured

WAYS TO GET STARTED

A thought to keep in mind when first getting started as well as after years of experiences is that "good teachers do not teach; they create exciting learning situations."[2]

---

[2]Steve VanMatre, *Acclimatizing* (Martinsville, Ill.: American Camping Association, 1974), p. 14.

Procedures

Make your first outings as simple as possible, using some of these tips:

> Start on a small scale. At first, spend a few minutes during a class period on the school grounds.
>
> Pick a subject area in which you already feel some competence and confidence. The selected activity should relate to ongoing study.
>
> Simplify logistics. Define the limits of your study area.
>
> Before your first environmental excursion, observe another teacher who is experienced in discovery and problem-solving approaches, if possible.
>
> Ask an aide or older student to help direct the activity.

Teaching Methods

A variety of approaches and ideas are possible, depending on age level, subject, objectives, and teacher abilities. The following methods will help you feel more prepared and comfortable.

> Find suggestions in books (including this manual) that can be used as a springboard to give relevance to your topic. Modify suggestions to meet your teaching needs.
>
> Once you have designed your outdoor experience, be flexible if an unplanned "teachable moment" occurs. Be prepared for weather changes and have an alternate plan.
>
> Teacher attitude is important in determining benefits from outdoor experiences. Be a willing colearner and discover with the students. Have a sense of wonder, and enjoy yourself.

KNOWLEDGE ABOUT THE NATURAL ENVIRONMENT

No one will ever know all there is to know about the natural environment. You do not have to identify objects outdoors before venturing forth. If you go outdoors for a special purpose, for example, to see a rock or to compare temperatures in different areas, you can go out feeling prepared for that particular experience by becoming familiar with the outdoor area and by reading brief background material in advance.

You will continually be learning with the students and should encourage them to look things up. The more you know about general ecological concepts, the more you will be able to make activities purposeful.

With a particular outdoor activity in mind, you need to know how to ask open-ended questions, make connections, and lead students to greater explorations. This comes with practice. The more you know about your particular topic for study, the more you can make connections. However, do not give right answers and names for things. Encourage students to find answers for themselves and to explore the how and why as well as what.

MINIMIZING DISCIPLINE PROBLEMS OUTDOORS

Getting started on a small scale with well-planned activities and clearly defined expectations can minimize behavior problems. The following suggestions will help maintain order. Involve students in planning and discuss behavior expectations in advance. Make sure students know what to expect and understand the assignment.

Be sure to plan activities that involve all students and that maintain their interest. Provide enough challenge, but not too much. Discuss problems with students after situations arise, and encourage desirable attitudes. Show how common sense rules make activities more meaningful.

Expect outdoor behavior to improve with student's experiences over a period of time. There is usually a brief time of getting used to the outdoors for study as well as recess. Students needing a lot of attention may benefit from playing an active role such as a special assignment that keeps them busy and earns them respect from classmates. Those who finish an activity early may need extra work.

Until the teacher gains confidence outdoors, a short experience and extra help can minimize problems.

ENVIRONMENTAL EDUCATION: INDOORS OR OUTDOORS

People approach teaching outdoors with a variety of preconceptions, orientations, and attitudes. Some teachers thrive in teaching beyond the classroom, and some take to it slowly and see it as an occasional technique.

Regardless of the amount of time spent beyond the classroom, the teacher will still use the classroom for most of the curriculum coverage. The teacher's attitude is as important indoors as outdoors in stressing interrelationships and making connections, in tying in experiences, and in providing practical applications to make concepts meaningful. How the teacher acts is as important, if not more so, than the information shared.

Discovery, problem solving, and inquiry approaches can be

used indoors as well as out. Interaction among students as well as with the teacher can be promoted to enrich learning within the classroom. A variety of materials, objects, and resources for handling, observation, and study within the classroom can increase environmental understanding. Community resources (such as people, maps, objects) can be brought into the classroom.

There are many environments within the school building (such as library, lunchroom, boiler room) that can be explored and compared.

First-hand experiences and learning by doing can take place anywhere, but there are more varied opportunities beyond the classroom. If only one experience outdoors is planned each week, it will heighten awareness and provide many examples of learning and involvement that can carry over and enrich the classroom studies.

If the teacher is not comfortable outdoors, an outdoor experience can be assigned as homework to be discussed or tested later within the classroom. Or the outdoor experience can be planned with help from aides or older students.

LEARNING DEVELOPMENT

Teachers need to understand students as well as subjects. This applies to all educational experiences, including environmental.

Although there are many theories about how students should be taught and what they should learn (process/content), it is generally recognized that learning takes place in three domains:

1. *Psychomotor* Manipulative and motor skills: using tools and coordination through body movement, vision, strength, speed, endurance and so forth
2. *Cognitive* Factual knowledge: specifics and how to deal with them through thinking, perception, memory, analysis, evaluation, and so forth
3. *Affective* Interests, attitudes, and values: how student receives and responds through feelings, sensitivity, motivation, open-mindedness, and so forth

Stages of Cognitive Development

According to Swiss child psychologist Jean Piaget, whose work has been receiving increasing attention of late, there are definite levels or stages of cognitive development that are characteristic of certain ages. Children can be in more than one stage at a time. New stages include the old and improve upon them, building upon previous knowledge and skills.

Sensory Motor From birth to about 2 years; beginning with reflexes and uncoordinated body movements and moving toward coordinated responses, both motor and perceptual; beginning of symbolic representation

> At this stage learning is through direct involvement in the environment, and many opportunities (safe) for exploring and interacting with the environment should be provided.

Preoperational From 2 to 7 years, approximately; egocentric thinking; sees one variable, one object at a time; is guided by intuition and perception; language develops; has not learned to make connections or to understand relationships; interest in what is real and immediate

> Environmental experiences increase child's natural curiosity and awareness of things. The greater the number and variety of experiences using the senses and dealing with objects, the more the transition to next stage can be encouraged.

Concrete operations From 7 to 11 years, approximately; still what is real; manipulation of objects very important; simple relationships begin; can make accurate observations, can measure and classify; beginning to use logic; can cope with more than one variable at same time and begins to relate parts to whole; begins to understand views of others and to show empathy

> Environmental experiences help in recognition of relationships between concrete things and between ordered events and in providing relevance to concepts. Children need concrete experiences in a variety of environments to encourage discovery, experimentation, and exploration to generate concepts.

Formal operations From 11 to adult; ability to observe, propose, analyze, evaluate, and make generalizations and hypotheses; abstract concepts can be understood in increasing complexity, building on past experiences of making predictions about variables and making connections; a concern with what is possible; ability to create new and unique thoughts

> Environmental experiences still provide a meaningful application of concepts, but now student can be increasingly involved in problem solving and decision making while investigating the environment.

Affective Development

The study of affective (emotional) development in relation to learning is limited in Piaget's theory. However, he did recognize that cognitive and affective development were two sides of the same coin and were interdependent.

Educational philosophers who have concentrated on affective development agree that a child's ability to move from one level of learning to another involves more than building on cognitive skills and concepts. Attitudes and values and social maturity help determine readiness as well. A child's self-image is closely related to learning motivation.

Environmental experiences can encourage the sensitivity, interest, and confidence that promote developmental progress. They can also encourage building values through group interaction and cooperative efforts.

Brief Guidelines for Teaching Different Age Levels

YOUNGEST   Students are interested in themselves and demand a lot of attention. They are curious, enthusiastic, eager to gain approval. Teacher needs to enjoy a variety of short activities, sensory experiences, and interpersonal relations. Teacher needs patience, the ability to help children to communicate, and a love of young children.

UPPER ELEMENTARY   Students are able to handle activities of longer duration with more involvement in choices. They work well in groups. Teacher needs to enjoy organizing a variety of activities that capitalize on this group's love of collecting information and exploring ideas and beginning ability to investigate and to put things into a frame of reference. Teacher needs to be able to detect differing patterns of growth and to encourage creativity. Teacher should be able to direct children in learning differences between fact and opinion, observations and personal values.

JUNIOR HIGH   The beginning of adolescence (generally junior high age) is a time of concern with developing values, moral reasoning, and judgment. It is also a time of great physical changes when the student is self-conscious and is interested in peer group approval. Teacher needs the ability to direct investigative processes creatively and to handle situations of personal interaction positively.

HIGH SCHOOL AND UP   Students can accept a growing amount of responsibility for organizing and developing their own learning projects. They are more sophisticated in research and analytic skills and mature in attitudes. Increasing intellectual challenges of students at this level make greater subject background necessary. Problem solving involving distinct contributions within the community is possible. However, students may lose motivation and need to regain a sense of involvement in their own learning processes. Confidence building is a teaching essential.

EVALUATION OF ENVIRONMENTAL EDUCATION APPROACHES

Environmental education is harder to evaluate than traditional learning because attitudes are involved in addition to the acquisition of knowledge. In environmental education the emphasis is on the process of learning through first-hand experiences, interactions within groups, creative explorations, and problem solving. Therefore, teachers need to organize the objectives of a study so that the process as well as the content, the how as well as the what, is evaluated.

Environmental experiences may be evaluated in a number of ways to determine whether learning has taken place. Traditional testing methods evaluate comprehension and memory through written or oral tests. In addition, the teacher needs to be able to observe attitudes, interests, value building, and interaction with peers in a variety of experiences within and outside of the classroom. The teacher can design tests that encourage different paths to an answer in order to recognize creativity. The student can become involved in self-evaluation. A more balanced picture of learning outcomes will result through many approaches to evaluating a student's environmental learning. These approaches can apply within any subject discipline.

INTEGRATING ENVIRONMENTAL EDUCATION INTO A SCHOOL SYSTEM

Ideally a K to 12 systemwide program, integrating environmental education into *all* subjects, should be implemented, involving all of the following components:

1. *Environmental education committee* Established by the school system and composed of administrators, teachers, students, and members of the community
2. *Environmental education coordinator* A full-time administrator to establish program goals with the EE committee and to oversee the operation of the program

3. *Curriculum development*   A K to 12 outline of concepts and skills for each grade level in sequential development
4. *Curriculum materials*   Units, resource materials, and information aids to meet curriculum needs
5. *In-service training*   Prepare teachers to use curriculum materials and community resources
6. *Training of citizens*   Citizens assist teachers and administrators as environmental aides, resource specialists, and so forth
7. *School site evaluation and development*   Provides outdoor resources in immediate environment
8. *Inventory*   Community resources beyond the school site
9. *Coordination with private and public environmental groups*   Support and contribute EE program. What local conservation areas and people are available for school use? What state guidelines and curriculum materials are already available?

More often than not, all of the above steps will not be taken at once. Many school systems will not accept a K to 12 program with a paid administrator until numerous small efforts have proven their worth and have laid the groundwork for a more comprehensive program. Therefore, efforts by administrators, teachers, and citizens in promoting any of the above will be in the right direction.

OUTDOOR ACTIVITIES

SPRING SENSORY WALK   **Purpose**   To explore the school yard, using all the senses, to discover signs of spring.

Preparation   Warn students to wear suitable outdoor clothing. If class is not already doing spring projects, a little discussion of spring as a season of new life and growth is good preparation.

Equipment   Plastic bag or collecting container for each student (may be reused on later trips); magnifying glasses to share.

Activity   Divide class into three groups with a teacher/aide for each (about eight or so to a group). Each group will go to a different area and should be aware of what they see, hear, smell, and feel. They are to bring back at least one item (in their container) found by using their senses. Examples follow.

1. *See*   New grass, buds, other signs of new life. Dead life such as old acorns, dried leaves from last year. Insects and other small animals or signs of their presence such as feathers, nest-

ing materials, galls. See shapes and patterns in clouds, trees, land

2. *Feel* Texture of bark, leaves; shape of stones—sharp, smooth, rough; feel dirt—soft, gritty, moist; feel pussywillows, prickers; feel with hands, nose, cheek

3. *Sound* Can students bring back a sound in a bag? Let them decide how they will share a sound they have heard. They can make believe and act it out or they can tell about an object that cannot be brought back.

4. *Smell* General smell of the air, special smells of plants, animals, rocks, dirt, skunk cabbage, tree blossoms, mint, flowers, pine needles, water in drain pipe

5. *Taste* Omit this from list. If the group leader is *sure* of the presence of an edible plant like dandelion, mint, wintergreen, or sorrel, she or he can pass samples around so students can compare reactions. Do not encourage students to taste on their own.

Teaching Tips Let the students discover and share among themselves. Use guidance and leading questions if necessary to get things going. Bring them back together after they have had enough time to be aware of their discoveries. Compare what each has found. Return any animals to original homes and bring the nonliving objects back to the classroom for a display and later discussion. Art work and music projects can also be used to supplement a sensory walk. Additional trips can be planned to concentrate on a single sense, for example, a silent walk to hear things or a feeling trip. Read stories about spring.

SEEDS **Purpose** To become aware of different ways seeds are formed and how they disperse; to understand that seeds need adequate space and proper growing conditions to survive.

Preparation Bring a bag full of samples of seed coverings for class to see in advance of trip: skin—fruit; pods—beans, peas, garden flowers; shells—nuts; husk—corn; and hull—grass. Look at the variety of seed coverings. Are all seeds covered? Try to have examples of some that would be found in the school yard during a seed hunt such as a variety of grasses, weeds.

Equipment Plastic bags for collecting seeds; magnifying glasses to share.

Activities Send students out individually or in groups to a specified area to hunt for seeds. Have them investigate the area carefully to discover different kinds of seeds; quantity of particular kinds; and how seeds travel (see Figure 4-1).

1. Have them collect a sample of each variety discovered.
2. Let them count the number of seeds one plant produces (e.g., a milkweed pod or dandelion flower); or the seeds from one apple; or check the number of maple seeds or oak acorns found under one tree. What would happen if every seed became a new plant? What does a seed need to grow (soil, water, sun, space)? Why are so many extra seeds provided by nature?
3. Experiment to observe how seeds travel. Blow on some seeds to see if they float in the wind or on top of water. Does the shape of the seed help it to fall to the ground? Do any seeds stick to their clothing? Do any remind them of familiar means of travel (e.g., parachute—milkweed or dandelion; hitchhiker—beggar's lice or burdock; slingshot or rocket—touchme-not or witchhazel)?

Return to a central point to compare collections and discoveries.

Follow-Up Further studies of seeds can take place in the classroom. Collected seeds can be saved for bird food and/or for planting in pots with garden soil. Some seeds need to be kept in a cool, dark place before planting in the spring. Students can keep a record of where the seeds came from, a description of the plant (or name if known), and notes on how long they take to grow. Seeds from fruit can be brought in from home (apple, orange, grapefruit) and dried on the windowsill before planting. Some dried seeds are

Figure 4–1   Seeds: Growth, Uses, Methods of Dispersal

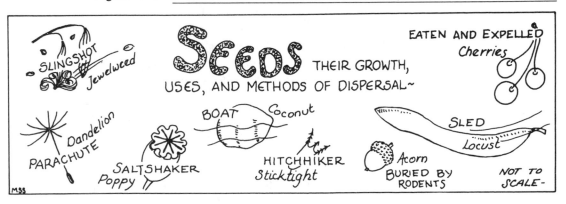

Reproduced by permission of MASSACHUSETTS AUDUBON SOCIETY, Lincoln, Massachusetts

edible (pumpkin, sunflower). Some seeds can be sprouted and eaten (beans).

ADOPT A TREE **Purpose** To observe a tree closely and to become aware of how it grows, changes, and relates to the environment.

Preparation Tree charts and posters can be on display in the classroom, and books about trees can be read or looked at. Begin in the fall so that there can be seasonal follow-up.

Equipment Magnifying glasses; plastic bags; tree notebooks, field guides for older students.

Activity Select a tree on the school grounds. (Older students—one for each or for a small group; younger students—select a class tree.) If there are not enough trees on the school grounds, get permission to use a nearby vacant lot. Students must try to find out as much as possible about their tree through sensory impression. Older students should keep records on their trees in addition, including the following:

1. *Shape of tree* Describe or draw a picture.
2. *Bark* Rubbing of bark—appearance and texture.
3. *Leaves* Describe or draw. Take a sample for checking in tree finder books.
4. *Twigs* Is formation on branch opposite or alternate? Twig shapes can aid in winter identification.
5. *Flowers* (seeds, fruit) Examine closely with magnifying glass.
6. *Life in or on trees* What kinds of interactions with other living things such as plant—moss, lichen, fungus or animal—insects, squirrels, humans?
7. *Environment* What does the tree take from earth and what does it contribute? What are its basic needs for survival?
8. *Condition* Is the tree healthy? How can you tell?
9. *Measurement* Measure size and shape and estimate height. Use English and metric measurements.

Younger students can get to know their tree as a friend. They can sit under it to read and make up stories about it. They can feel it, hug it, thank it, measure it with hand spans and arm spans.

Follow-Up Keep the record up to date through the seasons. Make displays of leaves, pictures, stories, and poems about class or individual trees. Carry through theme that a tree is a friend that helps the earth and people in related activities—art, dance, and music.

UGLY/BEAUTIFUL **Purpose**   To look at the school ground environment in terms of personal values; to encourage a sense of responsibility for caring for school grounds.

Equipment   Notebook.

Preparation   This can be a beginning school ground activity that does not require any subject background but is attitude building.

Activity   Students go out on the school grounds to look for things that are ugly and beautiful. Each student makes a list in a pre-scribed area for about 15 minutes. Come back into the classroom together where you make a compilation of results on the chalk-board. The master list includes one column for ugly and one for beautiful items. If an item gets put in both columns, it is removed to a third column representing difference of opinion. After every-one has had a chance to make contributions, discuss the items on which there is agreement and those on which there is disagree-ment. What are the reasons for the differences?

Follow-Up   The information can be categorized in different ways; for example, which items were man-made and which natural; which dead and which alive? Is there a correlation with ugly/beautiful? An additional value question would be to identify things students like or dislike on the school grounds. Discussions can lead to suggestions for improvement of the school grounds and for projects by individuals or the class.

INSECT INVENTORY **Purpose**   To explore and discover insects and their evidence on the school grounds. To observe insects in different stages of growth.

Preparation   Background on insect life cycles should precede this outdoor experience.

Equipment   Magnifying glasses; collection containers; trowels.

Activity
1. Divide students into three groups to look for insects (in egg, larva, pupa, nymph, or adult stages), and for evidence of insect life (bark beetle paths, anthills, wasp holes or nest, outgrown skins, leaves eaten, galls).

2. Each group goes to a different area of the school grounds. Within each area students check three different levels:
   a. Above ground (in the air; on trees or other tall plants; on the building)
   b. On the ground (on top, in, or under grass and leaves; under a stone; under or within a log)
   c. Under the ground (use trowel to investigate)
3. Students are to put specimens or evidence in container or to be prepared to describe insect if it escapes or might sting. The three groups come back together to compare what kinds and how many varieties are discovered in each area (and each level of the area). Some of the questions to consider include: Why were there more at one level than another? What kind of homes were observed? What might be their food supply? Who might eat them?
4. The students should return all specimens or evidence to their original locations, unless proper provision has been made for keeping them in the classroom.

MAPPING SKILLS **Purpose** To develop mapping skills through experience in the environment.

Preparation The parts and purpose of a compass can be reviewed in advance. The compass is a magnetized instrument for telling direction. It orients itself in a north–south direction. Demonstrate the circle of 360 degrees, with north at 0 to 360 degrees. Use chalkboard if available. If outdoors use eight children to form the circle. Let them determine degrees for NE, E, SE, S, SW, W, NW. This will be a review for many who have already had degree finding in math. The handling of a compass instrument may be new, however. Stress that the compass needle must always be oriented to north and held steady and level before starting in any compass direction. Make sure there are no metal objects (zippers) nearby to attract the compass needle. A landmark should be sighted in the direction you want to go (sight means to read degrees of direction) and then walk in that direction. This is easier than trying to follow the direction of the bouncing needle as you walk.

Equipment
1. Compasses and markers for compass activity
2. String and paper for recording pacing activity
3. Graph paper for maps

Activity 1. Compass Outside each student (or group) gets a compass and a marker (e.g., golf tee) and is assigned an area for practice. The student orients the compass, then walks 10 paces north, 10 paces east, 10 paces south, and 10 paces west. What

Figure 4–2.
Map Symbols

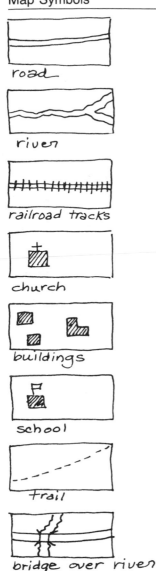

road

river

railroad tracks

church

buildings

school

trail

bridge over river

Figure 4–3.
Sample Pace and
Compass Map

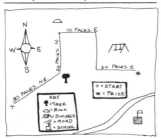

happened? Student keeps trying until he or she returns to the same spot as the marker. For those with extra time, variations of direction and distance can be given: for example, 10 paces NE, 10 paces SW, 10 paces SE, and 10 paces NW. Or 25 paces NE and so forth, which is more difficult.

Activity 2. Pacing Distance can be measured without using measuring equipment by finding the length of a pace. A pace is a normal walking stride, measured from heel to heel. Often it is the normal walking stride of two steps or everytime the same heel is recorded. Have students walk a distance of 100 feet, which has been laid out with string or other markers. Each student should walk this distance three times, counting the number of paces each time. Then figure out the average by adding the three pacing figures and dividing by three. Divide into 100 for the length of pace. Keep a record of each student's average so that the class average can be figured out later. Different areas of the school grounds can be measured with pacing and with use of a compass.

Activity 3. Map making Once the use of a compass and pacing are understood, students are ready to make a map. Review how information is put on a map through the use of landmarks and symbols. A *landmark* is a stationary object that is an identifying feature of the area mapped. It is large enough to sight with a compass and will not disappear, like a snow pile, by changing weather conditions or like a small rock, by moving it. To record landmarks on maps, *symbols* are used, with a map legend explaining what the symbols stand for, as shown in Figure 4–2. These special signs eliminate unnecessary writing or drawing all over a map and thus simplify reading it. Examples of common map symbols can be demonstrated.

Divide the class into two groups and give them written rules for making their maps and symbols. Each student should make the map as challenging as possible, and each group should select one map for the opposing team to follow. A prize can be hidden at the end of the route. See sample map in Figure 4–3.

1. Each map must contain at least 5 map symbols
2. Each map must contain at least 5 compass bearings
3. At least one of the 5 compass bearings must be NE, SE, SW, or NW
4. At least 100 paces must be used to get to the prize
5. The prize must be hidden from plain sight

Follow-Up Additional map-making activities can further develop mapping skills. The mapping of small areas on the school grounds can lead to a complete school grounds map with pacing distances related to a scale. Topographical maps can be studied to see how natural features and contours (elevation) are indicated. If there are maps of your areas, see if the students' observations agree with them. Elevation studies can be carried out, and a relief model of the grounds can combine all the information gathered.

REFERENCES

Teaching Environmental Education

ADULTS   Bloom, Benjamin B., and David R. Krathwohl. *Taxonomy of Educational Objectives: Handbook 1: Cognitive Domain*. New York: Longman, 1979.

Childress, R. B. "Public School Environmental Education Curricula: A National Profile." *Journal of Environmental Education*. no. 3 (1978): 2–11.

Dickey, Miriam, and Charles E. Roth. *Beyond the Classroom*. Lincoln, Mass.: Massachusetts Audubon Society, 1972.

Dinkmeyer, Don, and Rudolph Dreikurs. *Encouraging Children to Learn*. New York: E.P. Dutton, 1979.

Education Development Corporation. "An Overview of the Piagetian Levels of Development." E.D.C. Follow Through, Open Education Project. Newton, Mass., Feb. 1977.

Garigliano, Leonard J., and Beth J. Knape. *Environmental Education in the Elementary School*. Washington, D.C.: National Science Teachers Association, 1977.

Gross, Phyllis, and Esther P. Railton. *Teaching Science in an Outdoor Environment*. Berkeley, Calif.: University of California Press, 1972.

Pulaski, Mary A. *Understanding Piaget: An Introduction to Children's Cognitive Development*. New York: Harper & Row, 1971.

Roth, Charles E. "Citizen Assessment of Environmental Education." *Environmental Education Report* 2, 3 (1974): 1, 6–7.

Sale, Larry L., and Ernest W. Lee. *Environmental Education in the Elementary School*. New York: Holt, Rinehart and Winston, 1972.

Stapp, William B. *Integrating Conservation Education into the Curriculum (K-12)*. Minneapolis, Minn.: Burgess, 1965.

———and Dorothy A. Cox, eds. *Environmental Education Activities Manual*. Farmington Hills, Michigan, 1979.

Tanner, R. Thomas. *Ecology, Environment and Education*. Lincoln, Neb.: Professional Educators Publications, 1974.

Outdoor Activities: Spring Sensory Walk

CHILDREN   Beer, Kathleen Costello. *What Happens in the Spring*. Washington, D.C.: National Geographic Society, 1977.

Borland, Hal, and Anne Ophelia Dowden. *The Golden Circle. A Book of Months*. New York: Thomas Y. Crowell, 1977.

McClung, Robert M. *Peeper, First Voice of Spring*. New York: William Morrow, 1977.

ADULTS   Lawrence, Gale. *The Beginning Naturalist: Weekly Encounters With the Natural World*. Shelburne, Vt.: The New England Press, 1979.

Van Matre, Steve. *Acclimatizing*. Martinsville, Ind.: American Camping Association, 1974.

CURRICULUM GUIDE   Minnesota Mathematics and Science Teaching Project (MINNEMAST). *Using Our Senses*. Minneapolis: University of Minnesota, 1971. (K–3)

Outdoor Activities: Seeds

CHILDREN   Budlong, Ware, and Mark H. Fleitzer. *Experimenting with Seeds and Plants*. New York: G.P. Putnam's Sons, 1970.

Selsam, Millicent E., and Jerome Wexler. *Eat the Fruit, Plant the Seed*. New York: William Morrow, 1980.

CURRICULUM GUIDES   *Grow A Mini-Garden*. The Organic Classroom Series. Emmaus, Pa.: Rodale Press, 1971. (K–8)

Newcastle, Verne N. *Addison-Wesley Science*. Stem Series. Grade 2. Reading, Mass.: Addison-Wesley, 1980.

Outdoor Biology Instructional Strategies (OBIS). Set 1. "Seed Dispersal." Berkeley, Calif.: Lawrence Hall of Science, 1975.

Outdoor Activities: Adopt a Tree

CHILDREN   Cooper, Elizabeth K., and Padraic Cooper. *A Tree is Something Wonderful*. San Carlos, Calif.: Golden Gate Junior Books, 1972.

Cowle, Jerry. *Discover the Trees*. New York: Sterling Press, 1977.

Pringle, Laurence. *Into the Woods. Exploring the Forest Ecosystem*. New York: Macmillan, 1973.

ADULTS   Jackson, James P. *The Biography of a Tree*. Middle Village, New York: Jonathan David, 1979.

Outdoor Activities: Insect Inventory

CHILDREN   Cole, Joanna, and Jerome Wexler. *Find the Hidden Insect*. New York: William Morrow, 1979.

Milne, Louis J., and Margery Milne. *Insect Worlds*. New York: Charles Scribner's Sons, 1980.

ADULT   Bland, Roger, ed. *How to Know the Insects*. 3rd ed. Dubuque, Ia.: William C. Brown, 1978.

Minnesota Mathematics and Science Teaching Project (MINNEMAST) *Living Things in Field and Classroom*. Minneapolis: University of Minnesota, 1969. (This handbook is especially good on care of insects in the classroom.)

Zim, Herbert S., and Clarence A. Cottam. *Insects*. Golden Guide Series. New York: Golden Press, 1951.

Outdoor Activities: Mapping Skills

ADULTS   Kjellstrom, Bjorn. *Be Expert with Map and Compass*. New York: Charles Scribner's Sons, 1976.

CURRICULUM GUIDES   Examining Your Environment Series. *Mapping Small Places*. Toronto: Holt, Rinehart and Winston, 1972. (Grades 6–8)

National Environmental Education Development (NEED). *Adventure in Environment*. Student and Teacher Manuals. Morristown, N.J.: Silver Burdett, 1971. (Grades 5, 6)

5 · Field Trips Workshop

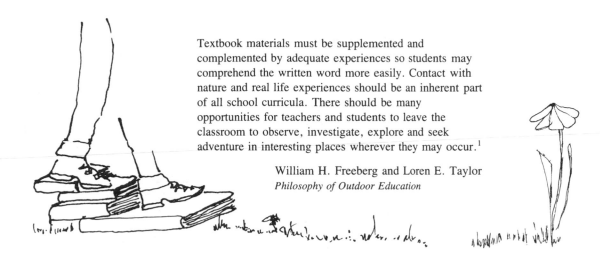

Textbook materials must be supplemented and complemented by adequate experiences so students may comprehend the written word more easily. Contact with nature and real life experiences should be an inherent part of all school curricula. There should be many opportunities for teachers and students to leave the classroom to observe, investigate, explore and seek adventure in interesting places wherever they may occur.[1]

William H. Freeberg and Loren E. Taylor
Philosophy of Outdoor Education

Goals

Field trips, properly planned and organized, can make opportunities available for individual discovery and group cooperation in the outdoor environment. They can provide valuable first-hand experiences that increase student awareness of the interdependence among all living things and encourage student responsibility for protecting the environment that supports life.

Procedures

Field trips can involve a 10-minute experience on the school grounds or a much longer excursion that calls for transportation, permission forms, and other details. The procedures outlined below are designed to cover all possible contingencies; many aspects can be simplified to suit individual situations. Whether the activity is a short one outside the door or an all-day safari, the following requirements should be considered.

---

[1]Minneapolis, Minn.: Burgess, 1961, p. 129. Reprinted by permission.

Who? The number of *students,* age group, and amount of prior outdoor experience will determine the length of the trip, the destination, objectives, and how much assistance is needed.

Parents should be informed about trips involving transportation, including objectives, requirements of students (permission slips, money, and proper clothing).

Adult assistance (teacher aides or adult helpers) should be secured ahead of time and briefed on role and details of trip.

What? Make sure there is a focus to the trip. Relate the field trip to ongoing studies. Do not make the trip an isolated experience or a "lark."

Where? Examine the site in advance to determine its learning opportunities, and do not rely on discovering something once there. The location should be close enough to reach comfortably, either by walking or by transportation. Check on parking space and any necessary reservation. If transportation is involved, make sure the route (maps for drivers are a good precaution) and itinerary are known by all. Check points can be established.

When? Start planning early enough to make all necessary advance arrangements. Allow time to prepare students in terms of subject, equipment, apparel, and any other aspects that affect them. Involve students in as much planning as possible.

How? These hints may be helpful once the planning is completed and the field trip begins.

Set ground rules in a positive manner. Remind students of the need to stay together within a limited area, to care for equipment, and to observe good conservation practices. A system of keeping track of students through buddies or division into groups should be worked out.

Do not walk too much. A tired group cannot learn. If you walk to reach your study site, plan activities along the way that will hold their interest and keep the group together, for example, a listening stop can provide a change of pace and ward off fatigue.

Do not talk too much. Lecturing can turn students off. Involve them in learning by doing.

Make your first outing short and work up to longer field trips. It takes time for you and the students to become used to the freer atmosphere outdoors. Frequent use of school grounds and nearby areas for short trips should prepare students for getting the most out of longer trips.

Do not stress identification. If students want to learn names, let them look in books. They can invent their own names using special characteristics of the items, or they can take a sample or, better still, a drawing back to the classroom to research.

Involve the entire class throughout. Encourage response through provocative questions and participatory activities designed to stimulate observation, inquiry, exploration, and discovery.

Equipment

Too much equipment can prove unmanageable. Bring only what you consider essential and can be carried in convenient bags such as shopping bags or knapsacks.

1. First aid supplies: bandages, burn aid, something for bee bites, bug repellent, and so forth. Extra supplies might be necessary if any students have special allergies or health problems.
2. Luncheon bags should include names.
3. Proper clothing should be stressed for the type of trips being taken, and provision should be made for rainy weather.
4. Trash disposal bags are essential.
5. Field guides, compasses, hand lenses, containers for samples to be returned to classroom, binoculars, and photographic supplies are all equipment that may be used for specific trips.

Follow-Up

Some of the many ways in which interdisciplinary classroom follow-up activities can reinforce the field experience are:

1. Have students write thank you letters to field study site owners, group leaders, volunteer drivers, and so forth.
2. Prepare notes and records of specimens, experiments, and activities.
3. Encourage displays of drawings, rubbings, photographs, and other visual reminders of the field experience.
4. Share findings with other classes and with parents through programs such as plays or audiovisual interpretations. Older students with field trip experience can teach findings to younger classes.
5. Refer to field trips frequently in class discussion when studies provide openings for comparison and analysis.

FIELD TRIP ACTIVITIES

The following activities are generally for upper elementary school children, but the concepts and activities can be simplified for younger children. For the earlier ages, sensory impressions and experiences in handling or observing objects should be emphasized. All activities can be carried out throughout the year, except for the soil and decay field trips, which are not suitable when there is snow or frozen ground.

ROCK FIELD TRIP

Purpose   To study rocks as an important part of the Earth structure and to understand what goes on around, on, and under them.

Preparation   Locate a site nearby that contains rocks. If necessary, use a rock in the foundation of the school building or wall. Before the field trip you may want to familiarize the class with the common rocks of your area, for example, granite in New England, sandstone in the southwest, limestone and slates in the New York, Pennsylvania, Ohio area. If you choose not to do this, you can still do the following activities.

Equipment   Magnifying glasses; field guides (for older students).

Activities   Have students each select a rock and examine it closely. They should think of all the ways to describe its characteristics, using all of their senses. The following are suggested activities to present to students.

1.   Consider how the rock got there. Is it bedrock (part of the rock foundation that is continuous all over the Earth) or is it a loose boulder? If loose, how was it carried to this site? Look for scratches that would indicate it had been scraped along under the glacier. Are there other similar rocks nearby from which it might have broken away?
2.   Look for veins of different materials that may run through the rock. Veins are a sign that the rock developed cracks because of movement in the Earth's crust or because of shrinking while cooling from the molten state. Melted rock intruded into these cracks or water deposited minerals as it flowed through the cracks.
3.   If flakes of mica are present, they are easy to scrape off. Sometimes crystals of other minerals stand out also.
4.   Can you see any signs of erosion or wearing away of the rock? What has done it: weather (freezing and cracking)? Water flowing on or by it? Or perhaps people's feet, if this rock is on a path?

5. Examine the plants on a rock. Lichens can grow on bare rock where other plants cannot get a footing. In cracks and ledges, dead plants and windblown soil collect and enable mosses to start growing. As the soil gets richer from the breakdown of these plants, other more extensively rooted plants are able to grow, and their roots crack the rock more.

6. Look for animals that live on or under the rock. Little cracks and holes often house insects, spiders, and their eggcases, and under damp edges toads and salamanders hide in wait for them.

Follow-Up Small samples of rocks can be brought into the classroom for close study. With very young children look for colors and shapes. Find pebbles that match big rocks. Older students may want to try simple identifications. Fossils are another follow-up to general rock study.

VISIT THE LOCAL CEMETERY

Purpose To use the cemetery as a community resource for understanding local history. To study gravestones as a primary source material.

Preparation You may need to acquire permission to enter a graveyard. Check to see if any activities such as grave rubbings are limited. Discuss cemetery rules such as rights of plot owners. A brief introduction to local history is helpful if the trip is not part of an ongoing community study.

Equipment Magnifying glasses; paper and crayon for rubbings; treasure hunt sheets for younger students and assignment sheets and graph paper for older students (optional).

Activities Take a trip to the oldest graveyard in your community. Divide the students into groups and give them assignments, which may include some or all of the following detective explorations, depending on age and time allowed.

1. Look for the oldest stones. What are the dates on them? How many years ago was this? How old were the people when they died? Do the stones look handcut? Look for the next oldest stones. Compare dates and types of stone with oldest.

2. Look for symbols or motifs on the early stones, and make rubbings or drawings of them. What do these symbols mean (death's head, weeping willow, urn)? Look for any other unusual features in the carvings such as initials or a biographical likeness of the deceased on the stone. Can you find any unusual sayings that tell something about the deceased?

3. Look for family names. Were there family plots in the olden

days? Are there today? What are some of the dominant family names? Are any of the same families still living in the community? Any of the same names on streets, buildings, areas? Are any names similar to students in the class?

4. Look for causes of death listed on the gravestones. Do many deaths at same date give evidence of smallpox or other plagues? How can you tell children's graves? Wartime soldiers' graves?

5. Landscape reading. Why do you think this spot was selected for a cemetery? Look at the terrain from all angles. Is there a difference in vegetation between older and newer parts? Look for stone walls. Older students can make a graph map of the oldest part of the cemetery.

Follow-Up   Gravestone rubbings can be displayed. Students can do research to find out local conditions at time of gravestone dates. Families can be studied in more detail, and oldtimers can be invited into the classroom to discuss old traditions and to teach crafts.

STUDY A ROTTING LOG   **Purpose**   To observe stages of decay and succession in the breakdown of a log into soil. To understand how a decaying log contributes to a living community.

Preparation   Find a site that contains more than one rotting log for investigation, and provide classroom background (depending on age) on plant and animal communities, food chains, and succession.

Equipment   Magnifying glasses, notebook (optional).

Activity   Have students locate rotting logs that are in more than one stage of decay, that is, one that is beginning to break down, one that is in an advanced stage of decay and has already contributed much to the ground humus, and so forth. Explain that the investigation will take place where the logs are found within a prescribed area. Divide the students into groups depending upon how many logs are found. Adapt the following activities to the age level with which you work.

1. Study the log as part of a tree. How did the tree die? If it was cut, are tree rings still evident? Can you tell what it once looked like? Are any similar trees located nearby? Are there any stump sprouts?

2. Study the log as a home for plants and animals. What is alive

within the log? What roles do scavengers play in breaking down the log. Do any predators eat the scavengers? (Look up words.) Can any food chains be suggested?

3. Study the log as contributing to the soil. As it decays, what happens?

4. Make a comparison of the different logs you find, and determine whether stages of succession are recognizable. Look for differences in appearance, texture, and types or organisms feeding upon them. (For older students.)

Teacher Tips   After students have studied the logs, be sure logs are put back in place carefully. Never tear a log apart. It is a home for living things.

Follow-Up   If you find a location that will undergo development, sample logs can be brought back into the classroom for follow-up study. Use magnifying glasses and microscopes for close inspection of specimens. Make charts and drawings of kinds of critters found, where they were in the log, what they do there. Additional decay and recycling studies can be done in the classroom with mold, fungus growth, compost.

CREATIVE WRITING   **Purpose**   To provide inspiration and motivation for creative writing through discovery and use of the senses in the natural environment.

Equipment   Magnifying glasses; notebook.

Activities   Take a creative writing "safari" to a natural area that offers a varied and inspiring landscape. Try one of these ideas, or take several trips and try more than one.

1. Blindfold students or have them close their eyes. Let students sit quietly a few minutes and take in impressions with all their senses, except sight. After blindfolds are removed, they can jot down notes of their impressions, including emotional responses to the experience. These notes can be written up in more complete form in the classroom.

2. Take a poetry trip. As part of a poetry study, students may bring in descriptions they like from any sources, such as newspapers, books. These can be single words, simple phrases, similes, and so forth. Take a walk to look for locations that match some of these descriptions. Encourage students to offer new descriptions and original comparisons. Find a good resting spot, and let the students write a poem

about this spot or an imaginary place, using some of the descriptions the class has evoked. Let the students use blank or free verse to encourage creativity.

3. Frame the picture. Let students take in the natural surroundings with all their senses, and pick a scene to frame. They can hold up their hands or move around an imaginary camera to make a frame. Encourage them to squint, widen eyes, blink, and look from different angles. A favorite scene can be captured, held in the mind's eye, and considered with all the senses before its key features, artistic and ecological relationships, and personal reactions are written down.

4. Creative writing themes can be imaginary or science fiction: "If I were ant" or "This location in A.D. 2000 will look like"; or observational: "My favorite tree"; or contemplative: "I wish" or "I used to but now"; or any other ideas that will extend the classroom writing assignment to the outdoors to encourage freer expression of senses, imagination, and wonder.

Teacher Tips   Small groups lend themselves to a more relaxed, friendly atmosphere. Aide(s) may be needed for this purpose. The teacher or aide(s) should be participants, not lecturers, and should encourage informality and sharing. For many this can remove the obstacles to writing that may exist within the four walls of a familiar classroom setting.

Follow Up   During later classroom work that builds upon the field trip ideas, try to reinforce the creativity and emotional responses as well as the writing skills. Whenever possible combine creative writing with other forms of expression such as music, art, and drama, as well as with sensory involvement in the outdoor environment.

STUDY A VACANT LOT   **Purpose**   To look at ecological relationships in an urban setting. To consider the impact of humans on their surroundings and how other life adapts to man-made changes.

Preparation   This trip can be an extension of plant and animal studies for younger students. Older students need background on interrelationships within habitats and communities (including people). Social studies background on neighborhoods in the city is also good preparation. In advance, locate a vacant lot within walking distance of the school, obtain necessary permission, and prepare data sheets.

Equipment   Magnifying glasses; data sheets for plot study.

Activities Visit a vacant lot near your school. Divide the class into groups and assign each a section of the lot as a minihabitat to study. The whole class comes back together after a prescribed period of time. Data are presented briefly on each plot of land. Then discuss the vacant lot as a whole, including the following relationships:

1. *Plants in your plot* Weeds, trees, shrubs. Types, variation, and approximate number. How do they survive in this setting? What special adaptations do they have to survive human impact? Look at roots, stems, leaves of plants.
2. *Animals in your plot* Both visible and evidence of past activity (types, variation, and number). How are animal needs met? How do animals adapt to human presence? Why does this habitat attract them? What food is natural? What is left by humans?
3. *Humans in your plot* Investigate the litter to learn about human habits and activities here. Are there signs of footprints, paths, automobile marks, refuse? Signs of past history? Evidence of previous buildings, old trashpiles, plantings? What are harmful environmental effects of human activity, including trash, air pollution, erosion? What benefits can you see from human activity?
4. *The plot in relation to the community* Why is the plot vacant today? Is it an eyesore, a neighborhood problem, or an asset? What are future plans for the lot? How could it be improved? Students can interview passersby and neighbors to get reactions. Older students can see if there is a neighborhood action group and/or government agency responsible for the maintenance of this and other vacant city lots.

Follow-Up Additional data comparison and study of interrelationships can be done back in the classroom. The plants and animals around a school can be studied in more detail. Older students can make simple maps of a vacant lot and the neighborhood it shares with the school. A plan for improving the lot can be drawn up.

STUDY A SOIL PROFILE **Purpose** To examine closely samples of several soils and to make observations and comparisons by using the senses. To understand how soil is formed and how it relates to the natural environment.

Preparation Investigate the site in advance to locate several areas with different soil types. Arrange to take along an extra adult or older student so class can be divided into small groups.

Equipment Shovels; white paper (oblong shape); white glue; magnifying glasses; and activities list for each group.

Activities Each group is assigned a different study area on the selected site. At each designated area the group decides where to cut the soil profile. Let students guess what the soil will be like. Once the location for the profile cut has been agreed upon, each student can take turns using the shovel. If the group is large, more then one cut for each study area can be done.

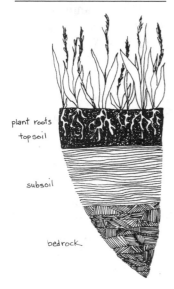

Figure 5–1
Soil Profile

plant roots
top soil

subsoil

bedrock

1. Have students make a V-shaped cut, with one side steep and the other gently sloped. It should be deep enough to expose different soil layers (1 to 2 feet usually), as shown in Figure 5–1.
2. Once the cut is completed, students should make observations about the texture, composition, color, and moisture in each layer. How does it feel at different depths? Have them "squeeze and ball it" and attempt to "ribbon" small samples. Let them describe sensations of cold, sticky, wet, gritty, and so forth. What do the samples smell and taste like? Notes can be taken on these findings and descriptions.
3. Students can study the amount of organic matter in the soil profile layers. How much undecayed and decayed material is present? Where did it come from? How is the organic matter breaking down? Look closely to see what is alive and what is dead in each layer. Were there animals in any or all layers?
4. Students can make a copy of the profile with a large piece of white paper smeared with glue. Press the glued side against the steep side of the cut and hold it there until soil layer samples adhere.
5. Make sure they carefully fill in the holes when the field activity is finished.

Follow-Up At the field study site a brief comparison of soil profile pictures can be made. In the classroom the profiles and field notes can be used to evaluate the experience in terms of what affects soil composition (weather, lay of land, vegetation, and animal life decaying) and how soil relates to the environment of an area. If small samples from each study area are returned to the classroom, let the students experiment with growing seeds in different types of soil and under different conditions. Try making soil (grind rocks, add water and decayed plant and animal material). Let them consider nature's time for a soil layer to be formed.

DIG A TRASHPILE **Purpose** To be able to use archaeological techniques to uncover material remains of the past. To observe, record, and analyze artifacts and features.

Preparation   Determine where you will dig, and make sure it is not a sensitive archaeological site. Check with local officials to see if there are any trashpits on school sites or other public lands that can be excavated, or consult the conservation or planning agency to find locations where development is about to take place. An old trashpile might be found near abandoned cellar holes or old boundaries such as stonewalls. Request permission of owner to dig.

Go over archaeological techniques including the use of the metric system, and prepare students for painstaking and meticulous work. Duplicate recording sheets for the summation of data. Students can help bring in supplies and make screens for sifting (one-quarter-inch mesh is good).

Equipment   String, stakes, measuring tape, plastic bags, and markers; magnifying glasses, compass; trowels, sifters, pails, toothbrushes, paint brushes; graph paper and data sheets.

Activity   Divide the class into teams of four to six. Give each team equipment, an equipment list and recording sheets. Set up a grid (squares adjacent to each other in a checkerboard pattern) or other plan for location of squares. Leave space between squares so that walls don't cave in and people aren't working too close together. Mark the grid or plan on graph paper, with squares numbered, and assign each team a numbered square (See Figure 5–2) of the trashpile to dig according to procedures outlined below or those in an archaeological guide.

1. Lay out a meter-square pit (100 cm × 100 cm) with metric tape or stick, string and stakes. Use compass so that N-S lines and E-W lines are parallel. Measure distance to a fixed point (datum point) and record on teacher's graph paper.
2. Dig one layer deep at a time (usually 10 cm. levels). Record information for each level separately. Mark bags with finds from each level, and divide according to: stone; ceramics; metal; bone and shell; and other.
3. Measure the square at each successive 10 cm. depth to make sure the walls are straight and the floor level.
4. Carefully skim the soil within each level with a flat trowel. Put soil to be sifted into a pail, away from the square. The sifted pile of one square should not be mixed with another. As large artifacts are found, they should be brush-cleaned and their position recorded before removal. Small pieces need only be sifted from the pail.
5. Stop digging at a depth of 50 centimeters unless artifacts or interesting changes in the soil are still being found. If anything other than the trashpile itself is uncovered, such as an old fireplace or part of a foundation, stop digging until an expert

Figure 5–2   Grid Plan of Trashpile

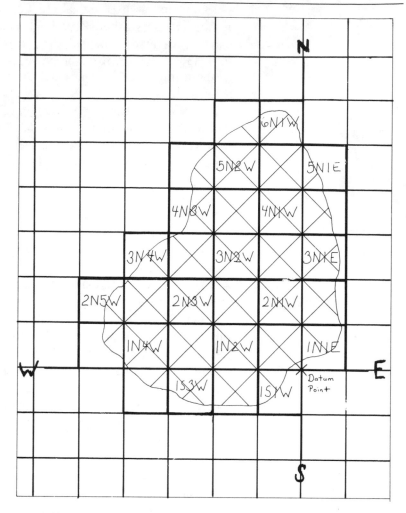

from an historical or archaeological society can be consulted. Move the group to another square and leave feature intact.

6. When all of the levels are completed, fill up the empty square with the sifted soil. Bring all artifacts, labeled and bagged, along with data sheets, back to the classroom for later analysis.

In addition to sharing the general work involved in completing the square, team members can be given specific jobs, such as the following:

1. *Soils scientist*   Records differences within and between soil levels and makes a soil profile of one wall of the completed square

2. *Artist*   Makes drawings of each level on graph paper, indicating the artifacts and their location
3. *Data recorder*   Writes down information on finds for each level, including descriptions of artifacts
4. *Baggy recorder*   Puts artifacts in plastic bags by categories and makes labels for each level
5. *Custodian*   Responsible for taking care of equipment
6. *Supervisor*   Sees that general work is shared and specific tasks are remembered

Teacher Tips   This can be one all-day field trip or several outings, if the location is nearby. The activity can tie in with ongoing studies of different cultures, and it can also be used to develop science skills of inquiry and analysis. Detective work can be done to understand the past through nonwritten information. Cultural resources such as old buildings, stonewalls, and trashpiles can be as important as recorded history. Tell the students why archaeological experts should be called in if any historic features or prehistoric (Indian) artifacts are found. Careless digging can destroy valuable information that is irreplaceable.

Follow-Up   When digging is completed, have the students wash, dry, and label artifacts, keeping them separated by levels. Each team of diggers should double check their data sheet to make sure all finds have been recorded. Make a large chart on which the information from all groups is combined. Discuss possible meanings the artifacts suggest. How long ago was this trashpile used? Decide on a period of time or range of dates when the materials were made and used. How were the artifacts used? What do they tell about former life-styles? Let the students use their imaginations in putting the pieces of the puzzle together, but have some good references on hand for researching historical periods, ceramic dates, and archaeological techniques. Make a classroom display of the artifacts and their stories. Invite a resource specialist to tell about the past history of the trashpile site.

REFERENCES

Conducting Field Trips

ADULTS   Mohr, Charles E. "How to Lead a Field Trip." Part of Audubon Teaching Aids, NB 2. New York: National Audubon Society, 1970.

Russell, Helen Ross. *Ten-Minute Field Trips*. New York: Doubleday, 1970.

U.S. Forest Service, Department of Agriculture. "Field Trips." Teaching Aid No. 4, Washington, D.C.: Government Printing Office, n.d.

Field Trip Activities: Rock Field Trip

CHILDREN   Pringle, Laurence. *The Hidden World; Life Under a Rock*. New York: Macmillan, 1977.
White, Ann T. *Rocks All Around Us*. New York: Random House, 1959.
————. 1963. *All About Rocks and Minerals*.
Wykoff, Jerome. *The Story of Geology*. New York: Western, 1976.

ADULTS   Pough, Frederick H. *A Field Guide to Rocks and Minerals*. 4th ed. Boston: Houghton Mifflin, 1976.

CURRICULUM GUIDES   Boyer, Robert E. *Rock Weathering*. Earth Science Curriculum Project Field Guide Pamphlet Series. Boston, Mass.: Houghton-Mifflin, 1971. (Junior High)
Freeman, Tom. *Layered Rocks*. Earth Science Curriculum Project Field Guide Pamphlet Series. Boston, Mass.: Houghton-Mifflin, 1971. (Junior High)

Field Trip Activities: Visit the Local Cemetery

ADULTS   Regional Center for Educational Training. *Perspective '75—Old Time Vermont and New Hampshire*. Hanover, N.H., 1976.
Swan, Malcolm. *Tips and Tricks in Outdoor Education*. 2nd ed. Danville, Ill.: Interstate Press, 1978.

CURRICULUM GUIDES   Antioch New England Graduate School. "Cemeteries and Cellar Holes." *Yankee Lands. A Land Use Curriculum Project*. Keene, N.H., 1980. (Junior and Senior High)
Project Kare. *The Cemetery: An Outdoor Classroom*. Student Handbook, 6th Grade. Blue Bell, Pa., 1974.

Field Trip Activities: Study a Rotting Log

CHILDREN   Selsam, Millicent. *Birth of a Forest*. New York: Harper & Row, 1964.

ADULTS   Massachusetts Audubon Society. "Deciduous Forest." *Curious Naturalist* XIII, no. 2 (1973).

CURRICULUM GUIDE   *Outdoor Biology Instructional Strategies (OBIS)*. "Natural Recycling in Soil." Set 1. Berkeley, Calif.: Lawrence Hall of Science, 1975.

Field Trip Activities: Creative Writing

CHILDREN   Amon, Aline. *The Earth is Sore: Native Americans on Nature*. New York: Atheneum, 1981.

Lewis, Richard. *Miracles. Poems by Children of the English-Speaking World*. New York: Simon & Schuster, 1966.

Sandburg, Carl. *Wind Song*. New York: Harcourt Brace Jovanovich, 1965.

ADULTS   Moffatt, James, and Betty J. Wagner. *Student Centered Language Arts and Reading. A Handbook for Teachers*. 2nd ed. Boston, Mass.: Houghton-Mifflin, 1976.

Teachers and Writers Collaborative. *Whole Word Catalogue 1. A Collection of Assignments K–12 for Stimulating Student Writing*. New York, 1975. (Excellent reference but out-of-print.)

————. 1977. *Whole Word Catalogue 2*. Creative ideas for elementary and secondary school.

Field Trip Activities: Study a Vacant Lot

CHILDREN   Adrian, Mary. *Secret Neighbors: Wildlife in a City Lot*. New York: Hastings House, 1972.

Annixter, Jane, and Paul Annixter. *Brown Rats, Black Rats*. Englewood Cliffs, N.J.: Prentice-Hall, 1977.

Rights, Molly. *Beastly Neighbors*. A Brown Paper School Book. Boston, Mass.: Little, Brown, 1981.

Simon, Seymour. *Science in a Vacant Lot*. New York: Viking Press, 1970.

ADULTS   Russell, Helen Ross. *Ten-Minute Field Trips*. New York: Doubleday, 1970.

CURRICULUM GUIDES   Minnesota Environmental Sciences Foundation. *Vacant Lot Studies*. Washington, D.C.: National Wildlife Federation, 1971. (Grades 5–9)

————. 1971. *Man's Habitat—The City*. (Grades 4–12)

Field Trip Activities: Study a Soil Profile

CHILDREN   Rhine, Richard. *Life in a Bucket of Soil*. New York: Lothrop, Lee and Shepard, 1972. (Excellent reference but out-of-print.)

White, William J. *An Earthworm is Born*. New York: Sterling Press, 1975.

ADULTS   Russell, Helen Ross. *Soil, a Field Trip Guide*. Boston, Mass.: Little, Brown, 1972.

CURRICULUM GUIDES   Foth, H., and H. S. Jacobs. *Field Guide to Soils*. Earth Science Curriculum Project Pamphlet Series. Boston, Mass.: Houghton-Mifflin 1971. (Junior High)

Minnesota Environmental Sciences Foundation. *Soil*. Washington, D.C.: National Wildlife Federation, 1971. (Grades 2–9)

Field Trip Activities: Dig a Trashpile

CHILDREN Evans, Eva Knox. *Archaeology. Secrets of the Past*. New York: Golden Press, 1969.

Porrell, Bruce. *Digging the Past*. Reading, Mass.: Addison-Wesley, 1979.

Weitzman, David. *My Backyard History Book*. A Brown Paper School Book. Boston: Little, Brown, 1975.

ADULTS Deetz, James. *Invitation to Archaeology*. New York: Natural History Press, 1967.

————. *In Small Things Forgotten: The Archaeology of Early American Life*. New York: Doubleday, 1977.

Robbins, Maurice. *The Amateur Archaeologist's Handbook*. rev. ed. New York: Thomas Y. Crowell, 1973.

Sullivan, George. *Discover Archaeology*. New York: Doubleday, 1980.

CURRICULUM GUIDE Antioch/New England Graduate School. "Cemeteries and Cellar Holes." *Yankee Lands. A Land Use Curriculum Project*. Keene, N.H., 1980. (Junior and Senior High)

6 · Nature and Ecology Workshops

> To the casual eye, one patch of woodland looks very much like another. This is far from true; the arrangement of trees in a landscape is precise and follows laws of bewildering complexity. Every forest is the outcome of an intricate chain of events in climate, earth history, soil development and many other factors—which have shaped the landscape and determined the kinds and numbers of trees growing there.[1]
>
> Peter Farb and the editors of Time-Life Books
> *The Forest*

THE PLANT WORLD

Living organisms are often divided into three kingdoms: animals, plants, and protista (neither plant nor animal). The plant kingdom is divided into phyla by structure and by method of reproduction. The lower phyla reproduce by spores, or simple methods, and the more complex phyla, the spermatophytes, reproduce by seeds. These seed-producing plants are subdivided into two basic categories: the conifers with naked seeds borne in cones (the gymnosperms), and flowering plants, with seeds protected within an ovary (the angiosperms). Figure 6–1 presents a plant classification chart.

Conifers have narrow needlelike or scalelike leaves and most of them, such as pines, firs, spruce, and hemlock, are evergreens. An exception is the deciduous larch.

The flowering plants include both woody types (mostly shrubs and trees) and nonwoody types (the grass and flower families). Most woody trees are broad-leaved and deciduous. Lumbermen refer to the deciduous trees as "hardwoods" and to the evergreens as "softwoods", but there are exceptions. For instance,

[1]New York: Time-Life Books, 1961, p. 9.

Figure 6–1   Simple Plant Classification Chart

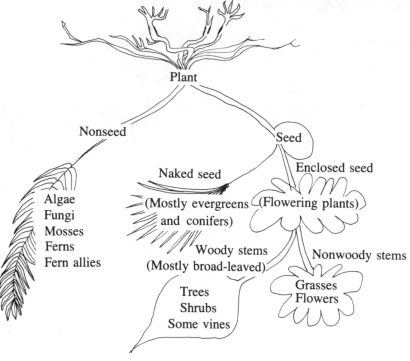

Plant

Nonseed

Algae
Fungi
Mosses
Ferns
Fern allies

Seed

Naked seed
(Mostly evergreens and conifers)

Enclosed seed
(Flowering plants)

Woody stems
(Mostly broad-leaved)

Nonwoody stems

Trees
Shrubs
Some vines

Grasses
Flowers

Figure 6–2   Identifying Features of Trees

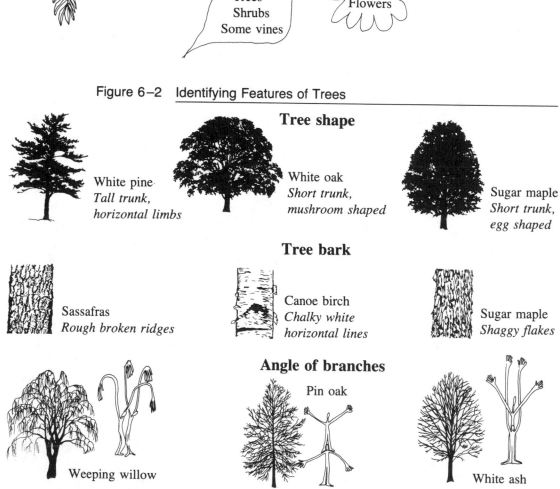

Tree shape

White pine
Tall trunk, horizontal limbs

White oak
Short trunk, mushroom shaped

Sugar maple
Short trunk, egg shaped

Tree bark

Sassafras
Rough broken ridges

Canoe birch
Chalky white horizontal lines

Sugar maple
Shaggy flakes

Angle of branches

Pin oak

Weeping willow

White ash

poplars and basswoods have soft, light, weak wood, and evergreen southern pines are harder than either of these.

Since trees grow nearly everywhere and are conspicuous year round, it is convenient to use them for plant study. In winter, tree bark and the angle of the branches are identifying features. In summer a tree can sometimes be identified by its shape. See Figure 6–2.

A *simple* leaf has one leaf on a single stem (see Figure 6–3), and a *compound* leaf has several leaflets on each stem (see Figure 6–4). Start at the very tip of the leaf and follow it down until you come to a *woody stem* of next year's bud (or bud location because the bud may be hidden between the woody portion and the stem). This is the leaf. You will notice that most leaves are arranged on the twig in one of two ways: alternate or opposite. Most trees have their leaves arranged in an alternate fashion, but there are four common families with opposite leaves: maple, ash, dogwood, and horse chestnut. (Acronym—MAD Horse.)

Figure 6–3   Simple Leaf Arrangements

Alternate   Opposite

Figure 6–4   Compound Leaf Arrangements

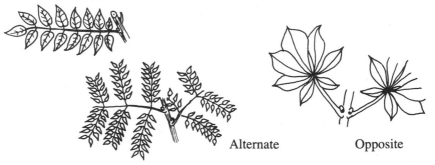

Alternate   Opposite

To study deciduous trees, take a close look at the leaves to determine how they are arranged and whether they are simple or compound. Remember—identification of particular species is not considered an end in itself. The process of identification, however, is a useful teaching approach because it develops the ability to recognize differences and to realize a sense of relationship among various plants. Use one of the books in the bibliography to key plants. It is fun to be a detective!

Twigs and buds may also be used to identify trees. In early summer buds are formed and remain on the twig until the following spring. See Figure 6–5.

Figure 6–5   Twig Parts

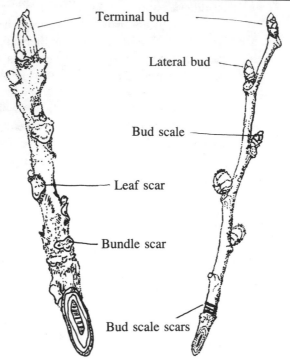

Terminal bud

Lateral bud

Bud scale

Leaf scar

Bundle scar

Bud scale scars

The following terms describe some twig parts that may be observed in the process of identification:

Terminal Bud(s)   At tips, usually larger than side buds
Lateral Bud   Along side of twig above leaf scar
Bud Scale   Protective covering for bud
Leaf Scar   Pattern left where the leaf stem was
Bundle Scar   Left within the leaf scar by the ducts to the leaf
Bud Scale Scar   Lines of rings left by last year's terminal bud
Bud scale scar to terminal bud   Distance twig grew the last season

PLANT ACTIVITIES

KEYING   **Purpose**   To become aware of similarities and differences between and among plants. To learn the process by which plants can be identified. This process can be applied to all things.

Equipment   Bag of assorted items for keying.

Activities   Explain to students that all keys are human inventions and are a convenient way of classifying things. In using a key, they must choose the characteristics of the items to be identified that will divide them into groups, one step at a time. The important thing in keying is that it be fun. Of course, the more information you have about the object you are trying to identify, the easier it is to form or to follow a key. Tree and plant guides include detailed information about the various parts of the plant in the front of the guide so that you can answer the questions accurately.

Approach keying with the students as if it were a detective game. Pretend the key guide is the detective who is searching for clues 'about the plant's identity and *you* must do the interpreting.

1. For example, in using Figure 6–6, first determine if leaves are (I) *Needlelike* or (II) *Scalelike*.

   a. If leaves are (I) Needlelike, proceed to (A) Leaves in bundles. If leaves are in bundles, are they (1) evergreen or (2) deciduous (dropped in fall), and so on.

   b. If leaves are (II) Scalelike, proceed in the same manner.

Figure 6–6. *Clues for Conifer Detectives* (Outline Form)

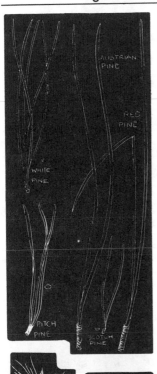

I. *Leaves needlelike*
   A. *Leaves in bundles*
      1. Leaves evergreen
         a. Five leaves in a bundle................White pine
         b. Three leaves in a bundle ....Pitch pine
         c. Two leaves in a bundle
            (1) Leaves 2" to 3" long, twisted, blue–green .... Scotch pine*
            (2) Leaves 3" to 6" long, stiff, do not break when bent...................... Austrian pine*
            (3) Leaves 4" to 6" long, break easily .... Red pine
      2. Leaves deciduous (dropped in fall)
         a. Many leaves in a bundle, twigs knobby ....Larch
   B. *Leaves single*
      1. Leaves flat, tips do *not* feel prickly
         a. Leaves ½" or less, on tiny stems, 2 white bands below; twigs rough after leaves fall ....Hemlock
         b. Leaves ¾" to 1", *no* stems; silver–white bands below; twigs smooth after leaves fall ....Balsam fir
         c. Leaves dark green above, yellow–green below; fruit red, berrylike; a shrub ....Yew
      2. Leaves not flat, grow all around twig, tips prickly
         a. Leaves usually 4-sided; can be rolled in fingers; twigs rough after leaves fall ..... Spruce
         b. Leaves ¼" to ½", one side gray–white, the other side green; fruit blue, berrylike, a shrub ....Pasture juniper
II. *Leaves scalelike*
   A. Branchlets flattened, fan-like sprays; cones ½" long, oblong .... Arbor vitae
   B. Branchlets not flattened; young leaf tips feel prickly, old ones do not; fruit blue, berrylike .... Red cedar

*Introduced species

Figure 6–7   Fruit Key

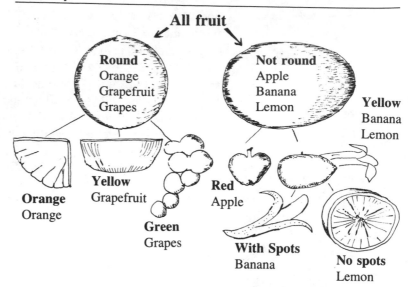

c.   Remember that the tree holds all the information. All you have to do is answer the questions accurately.

2.   Fruit in a refrigerator can be sorted in a variety of ways, for example, by color, or shape, or texture. Students can use the fruit key in Figure 6–7 to sort fruit.

Teacher Tips   Keys are used only as a method of teaching. They should not be used as an end in themselves because names should not become the focus of learning. The stress is on *relationships*. Young students can make keys using groups of objects that are familiar to them.

FOREST/SKYSCRAPER COMMUNITY

Purpose   To examine the forest community layer by layer, making each level analogous to the layers of a city skyscraper.

Equipment   Paper, pencils, drawing paper or matboard.

Activities   The six layers of the forest are broken down as illustrated in Figure 6–8:

The following questions can be asked about the forest/skyscraper community:

1.   *What animals are active in a particular area?* Look for birds in the understory; insects on many layers; earthworms underground, and so forth. Does there appear to be more activity on the forest floor than in the canopy? Why? Where is most of the activity in the skyscraper? Why? Animals who live in the forest have specialized means of locomotion to get there, for

example, wings, claws. How do people get to a penthouse if not by their own locomotion? (Elevators, electric stairways, and so forth.)

2. *Which layer of plants in the forest uses most of the sun's energy?* Though the canopy receives most of the sunlight, the amount and type of plants that grow below the canopy can be determined by the amount of sun they receive. Shade-loving plants will live in the dense forest while plants that do well in light but do not require direct sun will live in the more open forest. The diversity and quantity of the lower levels of the forest will determine how many animals can live there. Likewise, the skyscraper with a grocery store on the street level is more convenient to live in than one that does not have one. The penthouse of the skyscraper receives most of the sun's rays and tends to block the sun from lower levels. There are areas in cities so congested with skyscrapers that sun shines on the street only when it is directly overhead. How does this affect the temperature below? Can plants grow on the street level? Are members of the skyscraper community dependent on sunlight for food? Why? Can sunlight limit people's occupation of any layer?

3. *Who are all the animals who live in each layer?* You do not have to know names, just describe the *kinds of animals.* If you cannot see any animal, write down the ones you think would be able to survive (find both food and shelter) in that layer. What types of people live in the various levels of the skyscraper? Do different levels attract different types of people?

4. *Would there be more animals active in spring than in winter or fall?* Why? In a temperate zone (warm summers, cold winters) animals try to keep warm as much as possible in winter. Birds go south, insects crawl into the barks of trees and into cracks in the concrete, frogs bury themselves in the mud and people stay inside their skyscrapers. Do people stay more active than do other animals in winter? Why?

5. *Is there an advantage to a multilevel community?* In the forest as well as in the city the various areas of the community allow a greater diversity of organisms to live together, thus producing more items to exchange and share. In the skyscraper, there are often people living on the upper levels and stores and services on the lower levels. Can you think of other advantages or disadvantages?

6. *What kind of debris is on the forest floor?* Are there holes there? Who lives there? When leaves from deciduous trees and shrubs (those that fall off each year) fall to the forest floor, there are numerous plants and animals such as fungi, lichen, molds, bacteria and earthworms waiting to feed on the debris. They decompose the fallen leaves, animals, and logs and turn

Figure 6–8   Forest/Skyscraper Community

Forest	Skyscraper	
1. Canopy	Penthouse	This is where the leaves of the tallest trees form a roof for the forest.
2. Understory	Middle floors	This is where you will find the smaller hardwood trees.
3. Shrubs (4 to 8 feet)	Lower floors	This is a sparse area in the evergreen forest but can be too dense to pass through in the deciduous forest.
4. Herb layer	Mezzanine, shops	This includes the green plants with soft stems and usually shows more seasonal change.
5. Forest floor	Lobby, streets	This is the busiest layer and is composed of all the debris from the outer layers.
6. Underground	Basement	This area contains all the inhabitants of the soil. Some are there for temporary shelter, and others are working to break down material on and under the forest floor.

it into soil, which in turn enriches the forest and encourages new growth. Animals often live in the cool earth under the forest floor. Is there more activity on the street level of the skyscraper than anywhere else? What happens to people's litter? Does it land on the street level? Do the same organisms come to decompose it? Why?

Teacher Tips

1. These activities work well in an urban area where students can identify with the levels of the skyscraper. It may be done using pictures of forests, though a visit to a small forested area is always preferable.
2. It is best to ask questions at the site, discuss possible answers, then return indoors to write or sketch information observed about each layer.
3. The activity works well if groups are assigned various layers to examine. A story or mural of the combined groups' observations can be made and displayed.

COMMUNITIES AND
HABITATS

Purpose   To introduce students to a variety of plant communities and habitats and the plants within them.

Equipment

Activity 1.   Yarn, sticks.
Activity 2.   Paper and pencil.
Activity 3.   Paper and pencil.

Activities

1. *Habitat*   A patch of grass may look as if it contains nothing but grass. However, a variety of plants may be growing in a very small area. Put a circle of bright colored yarn on the ground and ask each student to place a stick in the ground beside each plant type, including different types of grass. Compare with other areas.
2. *Change*   Students can compare two trees of the same kind and record when they change color. Do the leaves fall at the same time? In autumn chlorophyll in the leaves begins to break down and the green color disappears. Yellow is always present in the leaves and will appear soon after the green disappears. Reds are from sugars that are left in the leaf. As the leaf ceases to make food, a corky layer of cells is produced by the tree between the leaf and the twig, which then cuts off sap flow. This protects the new bud until the following year. The leaf will eventually fall off the twig by its own weight or by wind and rain.
3. *Field notes*   Students can keep a pictorial or written diary of changes in trees throughout the year. Have them pick one

tree of their own and "adopt" it for the year. Remind them not to forget to look for visitors to their trees or for inhabitants of the bark, leaves, and branches.

4. *Decomposition* Green plants produce food and shelter for many animals during their growing season. They continue to provide nourishment and shelter for many smaller animals after they have fallen to the ground. Students look at a layer of fallen leaves, logs, branches, and so forth, on the forest floor. How thick is the layer of debris? Do they think this layer of natural litter is thicker in a northern forest than in a southern forest? Why? It is thicker in the North because in the South fewer leaves fall off the trees each year and there are not as many creatures in the soil to eat or decompose the litter. Why are there fewer animals? Because the weather is warm and the season is much longer for animals to remain active. Students can dig into the layer and see if they can figure out what food is for what animal. What is being used for shelter? What is being used for food?

5. *Nonflowering plants* See how many kinds of fungi students can find growing in the forest. Have them draw pictures of them. Feel them but do not remove them. Instead each student may "adopt" a mushroom to watch. Is it soft or hard? Does it have seeds? What happens to the mushroom in winter? Does anything eat the mushroom? Fungi include mushrooms and the various kinds of brackets and shelves that grow on decaying wood.

6. *Interdependence* Have students look for lichens growing on stones, logs, the sides of trees, and so forth. Ask them who they think would eat the lichen? Can they find half-eaten lichen lying around? A lichen is a combination of an alga and a fungus that is growing together. The alga is the green plant portion and does the photosynthesizing; the fungus obtains nutrients from the alga, while it is protecting it and keeping it moist. It is a mutually satisfactory relationship. Lichens grow on rocks and can survive in severe conditions, which make them an important pioneer plant.

7. *Examine needles of evergreens* Ask students how the needle shape helps trees survive winter? When the ground is frozen, trees cannot get much water. If water evaporated from leaves but was not replaced from the ground a tree would die of thirst. A thin needle shape reduces the area from which water can evaporate. How does the texture of the needle help the tree to survive winter? It is the hard waxy coating that reduces water loss.

8. *Students should observe and sketch* different kinds of *leaf scars* on twigs of deciduous trees. Leaf scars mark the point at which the circulatory system of the leaf was "shut off" as

the tree prepared to drop its leaves in the fall. Dark spots within the scars are ends of sealed-off vessels. Does the size or shape of the scar tell you anything about the leaf?

9. *Which is more flexible, the evergreen tree or the deciduous tree?* Tell students to try bending (without cracking or breaking) small branches of an evergreen tree and of a deciduous tree. (Different groups of students could compare different pairs of trees.) Which has more flexibility in the branches? Why? Evergreens (softwoods) need to be more flexible to "give" under a great amount of snow and ice. Deciduous trees (hardwoods) do not hold as much snow and ice on their branches.

10. *Find as many different kinds of winter buds as possible.* Instruct students to look on bushes as well as on trees. Are some covered with strong scales? Are some waxy? Are some sticky? Are some fuzzy? These are various forms of protection against freezing temperatures and drying winds.

11. *Look for cones of pine, spruce, hemlock, or fir.* Ask students if older cones are more open than newer ones? Alternate freezing and thawing causes scales of cones to open and to release the seeds that grow between the scales. Tell them to look on pine cone scales for the indentation where the seed was located. Put cones in water. The scales will close. Let them dry out and see what happens.

Teacher Tips Walks in the outdoors at any time of the year allow easy exploration of plant communities and change. Winter change can be dramatic, and this season should always be included.

WILD FOODS **Purpose** To gather and prepare edible wild foods high in nutritional value. To explore edible wild plants as a potential food source.

Preparation Select plants to introduce to class and know where they can be collected (enlist the aid of a local naturalist). Share a well-illustrated wild foods guide with the class before going out. Make sure students are familiar with poison ivy and other poisonous plants. Obtain permission to collect plants. Be sure the area has not been sprayed with any kind of herbicide.

Equipment
Activity 1. Container, sharp knife for you.
Activity 2. Container, pot, sieve, sugar, cornstarch.
Activity 3. Container, glass jar, boiling water, lemon, sugar.

Activities   Many plants considered weeds, such as cattails, w͟ collected and eaten by the Indians long ago and may be part of th͟ basic diet elsewhere today. Other weeds, such as violets, dandelions and purslane were brought over by European colonists who cultivated them in kitchen gardens. These plants, which are no longer favored, have escaped to roadside areas and lawns. All cultivated plants were once native to some part of the world, and there are many reasons why some are cultivated and others are not. For example, some are particularly tasty; some are adaptable to local soils and climates; or some are just peculiar to certain cultures. It is helpful to know that parts of plants that grow wild are also a potential food source.

1. *Salad greens* are rich in vitamin A and essential to a well-balanced diet. While lettuce, parsley, and spinach are among the many cultivated green vegetables you eat, our front lawns, schoolyard, and fields produce a variety of edible greens like dandelion and purslane (see Figure 6–9).
    a. Have students collect dandelion leaves in spring before the flower stalks appear. Cut the leaves at the base, wash them thoroughly, and boil them with butter, or prepare them raw in a salad. Remember not to dig from a lawn that has been sprayed with weed killer!
    b. Students can collect purslane from bare dry soils in fields and gardens. The entire plant, leaves and stalk, can be gathered from spring until fall and eaten raw in a

Figure 6–9   Dandelion and Purslane

salad or boiled and served with butter. Purslane and dandelion in combination make a wonderful spring salad.

2. *Rose hips,* the seedy fruits of rose blossoms, are rich in vitamin C. (Figure 6–10) They are collected in late summer but remain on the plant throughout the winter. People who live in woods often collect rose hips in winter as a survival food since they are quite tasty raw. Rose hips vary from the very tiny *Rosa multiflora* to the large *Rosa rugosa,* which flourish along the seashore. Rose hips make a nutritious soup, which you can make with students. Pick two cups of rose hips and boil them in a quart of water until tender. Put the mixture through a sieve to remove the seeds and skins, add more water to make a full quart, and stir in one-half cup of sugar. Reheat the mixture and thicken with one tablespoon of cornstarch. Stir the mixture until the soup looks clear.

3. The *tiny purple flowers of the common blue violet* (Figure 6–10) can be found in fields, in lawns, and by the roadside. Violets are rich in vitamin C and can be made into a tasty syrup in the classroom. Fill a glass jar with violet blossoms, cover them with boiling water, and seal the jar. Allow the mixture to rest for 24 hours. Strain off and discard the blossoms, and add the juice of one-half lemon and 2 cups of sugar to each cup of extract. Spoon the mixture over sherbert or add it to a glass of ice water for a refreshing drink.

Follow-Up Determine the origin of some wild plants and their past uses. Investigate the common names of plants for clues to their origin and use. For example, do Jerusalem artichokes come from Jerusalem? And are they artichokes?

Figure 6–10   Violets and Rose Hips

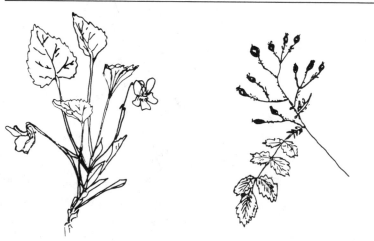

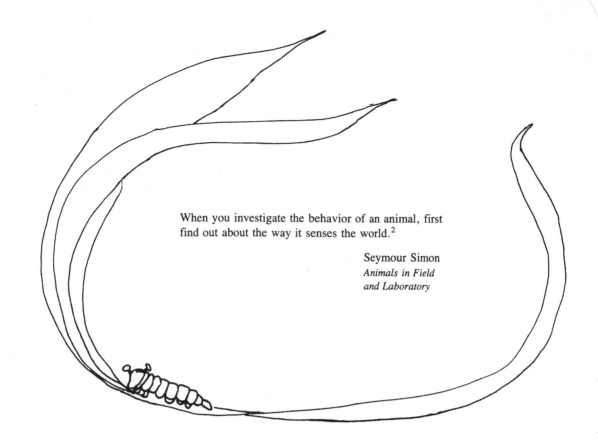

When you investigate the behavior of an animal, first find out about the way it senses the world.[2]

Seymour Simon
*Animals in Field
and Laboratory*

THE ANIMAL WORLD

The animal world is extremely large and includes more than 1 million species. They vary in size from the one-celled protozoa to the complex multicelled mammals. Regardless of size, however, animals can be distinguished from plants by some of the following characteristics.

1. Animals cannot produce their own food; therefore, they are all consumers.
2. They are all mobile at some stage in their life and can swim, fly, hop, jump, run, and so forth. (Only a few of the most primitive plants have mobility.)
3. Most animals have a nervous system.
4. They continue to grow over most parts of their body until maturity. (Plants, especially larger ones, grow from the tip outward.)
5. Most animals have cell boundary membranes that are delicate. The exception are sponges that are multicelled. (Plants have thick cellulose walls to hold cells.)

[2]New York: McGraw-Hill, 1968, p. 10.

This workshop will not attempt to deal with the entire animal world. Members of the lower phyla, such as the protozoa, coelenterates, flatworms, and roundworms will not be covered. (Only the earthworm, phylum Annelida, which is a favorite, is included in activities.) The higher order animals, the vertebrates and arthropods, which are easy to find, common to all parts of the country, and are best known to all of us, will be considered.

To aid in classifying animals, zoologists first divide them into broad general categories, then into more specific ones, for example,

Animal kingdom
Phylum (large animal group)
↓
Class
↓
Order
↓
Family
↓
Genus
↓
Species

Two of the larger phyla—Chordata and Arthropoda—which contain the most familiar animals, are shown in Figure 6–11. Any general zoology book will provide a complete family tree.

Phylum Arthropoda

Arthropods make up 85 percent of the total number of species in the animal kingdom. This makes them readily available for study. They are easily recognized because they have segmented bodies

Figure 6–11   The Arthropoda and Chordata

Figure 6–12   Phylum Arthropoda

Class	Crustacea	Arachnida	Insecta	Diplopoda
Examples	Lobster and crabs Shrimp Daphnia Sow bugs Beach flea	Horseshoe crab Spiders Ticks Mites Scorpions	Insects	Millipedes
Number of body parts	3	2	3	2
Pairs of legs	5 (at least)	4	3	2 (per segment)
Pairs of wings	—	—	1–2	—

and jointed feet. They all wear their skeletons on the outside. Thus, in order to grow they must shed their skins, or *molt*. Within the Arthropoda phylum four of the most common classes include the insects, Insecta; ticks and spiders, Arachnida; millipedes, Diplopoda; and lobsters, crabs, and sow bugs, Crustacea. See Figure 6–12, Phylum Arthropoda.

Metamorphosis, or change in body form, is characteristic of many invertebrates including most orders of insects. The following illustrates two forms of metamorphosis. (See also Figure 6–13, Ten Common Insect Orders.)

Complete metamorphosis = egg→larva→→pupa→adult

Example   A caterpillar hatches from its egg and eats until it grows so big its skin splits and it emerges with a new and bigger skin. After several such molts, it either splits its skin and a chyrsalis (case) is left or it spins a cocoon to enclose itself. In each instance the insect goes through the reorganization of its body into the adult form. When the change is complete, an adult (butterfly or moth) emerges to mate and lay eggs for the next generation.

Incomplete metamorphosis = egg→nymph→adult

Example   A little grasshopper hatches from the egg lacking wings; it eats, grows, and splits its skin, emerging with longer wings each time until it finally reaches adult size and structure.

Figure 6–13   Ten Common Insect Orders

TEN COMMON INSECT ORDERS

COMPLETE METAMORPHOSIS

WINGS DEVELOP INTERNALLY 4 STAGES

EGG ⊙
LARVA
PUPA
ADULT

GRADUAL METAMORPHOSIS

WINGS DEVELOP EXTERNALLY 3 STAGES

A) Young do not resemble adults

EGG ⊙
NAIAD
ADULT

B) Young resemble adults

ORDERS	METAMORPHOSIS (change during growth)	MOUTH	FIELD MARKS	EXAMPLES
ORTHOPTERA "Straight-winged"	Gradual change 3 stages	Chewing	FW leathery	Grasshoppers Crickets Cockroaches Mantids
HEMIPTERA "Half-winged"; two suborders as follows:				
HETEROPTERA "Varied-winged"	Gradual change 3 stages	Piercing-sucking	FW leathery at base thinner at extremities.	Stink & Squash Bugs Boatmen Backswimmers
HOMOPTERA "Wings-alike"	Gradual change 3 stages	Piercing-sucking	Wings clear or leathery FW form roof over HW.	Cicadas Aphids, Leaf & Tree Hoppers Spittlebugs
EPHEMEROPTERA "Ephemera-winged"	Gradual change 3 stages	Non-functioning in adults	Wings delicate, many cross veins; nymphs aquatic.	Mayflies
ODONATA "Toothed" (mouth parts)	Gradual change 3 stages	Chewing	Long, slender insects with long, clear wings. Nymphs aquatic.	Damselflies Dragonflies
NEUROPTERA "Nerve-winged"	Complete change 4 stages	Chewing	Wings equal in size with many fine veins. Clear.	Ant-lions Lace-wing flies.
TRICHOPTERA "Hairy-winged"	Complete change 4 stages	Sucking Larva: chewing	Wings covered with long hairs; Larvae aquatic, often in cases.	Caddisflies
LEPIDOPTERA "Scaly-winged"	Complete change 4 stages	Siphon-sucking Larva: chewing	Wings covered with scales.	Moths Skippers Butterflies
COLEOPTERA "Sheath-winged"	Complete change 4 stages	Chewing	FW horny, meeting in straight line down back over HW.	Potato & Lady Beetles Fireflies
HYMENOPTERA "Membrane-winged"	Complete change 4 stages	Chewing Lapping Sucking	FW larger, HW often hooked to FW or no wings.	Wasps Ants Bees
DIPTERA "Two-winged"	Complete change 4 stages	Piercing-sucking or Sucking	One pair of thin transparent wings.	Gnats Flies Mosquitoes Craneflies

FW — Front wings   HW — Hind wings

EGG   NYMPHS   ADULT   3 STAGES

mss

Phylum Chordata

Vertebrates are the animals with backbones and nerve cords down their backs. Their skeletons are internal in contrast to the arthropods whose skeletons are external. The vertebrates include fish, amphibia (frogs, toads, and salamanders), reptiles (turtles, snakes, and lizards), birds, and mammals.

Fish, amphibians, and reptiles are cold blooded, which means their body temperatures are not internally regulated but fluctuate with their environment. When the environment's temperature drops, their activity slows down and their respiration and heart beat become very slow. They survive winter by going below the frost line or into water that does not reach freezing temperatures.

FISH   Fish make up the largest group of vertebrates. In fact, there are more species of fish than all the other vertebrates combined. Moreover, primitive fish were the ancestors of all the vertebrates known today. (See Figure 6–14, Classes of Fish.)

Figure 6–14   Classes of Fish

Class	Features	Examples
Agnatha	Without true jaws or limbs	Lamprey
Chondrichthyes	With cartilaginous skeletons and exposed gill slits	Sharks and rays
Osteichthyes	With bony skeletons, covered with gill slits and rayed fins	Common fish, i.e., trout, salmon, perch, cod

AMPHIBIANS   Amphibians (frogs, toads, and salamanders) were the first animals to venture out of the water. Even today their degree of adaptation to land life is variable and limited. Their jelly-covered eggs are deposited in or near the water and hatch into gilled, plant-eating larvae or tadpoles. When these mature to air-breathing carnivores, they may or may not live on land, but they definitely return to the water to mate and lay eggs.

REPTILES   Reptiles (turtles, snakes, lizards, chameleons, alligators, and crocodiles), whether terrestrial or aquatic, have lungs instead of gills, breathe air, and are less tied to the water. However, they are still cold blooded and must protect their bodies from temperature extremes. As a result many species live underground or in the water or feed at night in order to avoid high and low temperatures. The characteristics of reptiles and amphibians are outlined in Figure 6–15. Some salamanders, toads, and frogs may be identified using Figure 6–16, Adult Amphibians of Massachusetts, and some snakes may be identified using Figure 6–17, Adult Snakes of Massachusetts.

Figure 6–15   Amphibian and Reptile Characteristics

	Amphibians	Reptiles
Examples	Toads, frogs, salamanders	Snakes, lizards, turtles, chameleons, alligators
Skin	Moist and smooth or dry and warty	Dry, scaly
Claws	None	All except snakes
Respiration	Gills when young Lungs when adult Skin plays a small part	Lungs
Reproduction	Eggs laid in water (occasionally under wet debris on land)	Eggs laid on land
Young	Tadpoles in water	Same as adult

Figure 6–16   Adult Amphibians of Massachusetts

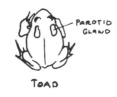

PAROTID GLAND

TOAD

I.   *With a tail*... Salamanders—(A)
II. *Without a tail*
    1.   Skin dry and warty, parotid gland behind each ear... Toads—(B)
    2.   Skin damp and smooth, no parotid gland ....Frogs—(C)
A.   *Salamanders*
    1.   *Four-toed* (four-toed hind feet and front feet), orange-brown above, white below ...Four-toed S.
    2.   *Five-toed* (five-toed hind feet, four-toed front feet)
       a. *Brook* salamanders,
         (1)   *Yellow body* with two blackish lines ....Two-lined S.
         (2)   *Light reddish body* with mottled darker tones....................................Purple S.
         (3)   *Blackish body,* peppered all over with tiny whitish spots, stout, tail keeled above .... Dusky S.

b. *Land* salamanders,
   (1)   *Blackish body*
      (a) Peppered all over with tiny whitish spots, slender, tail rounded above (black phase) .... Red-backed S.
      (b) Wide reddish striped down back (red phase) .... Red-backed S.
      (c) Wide black and white bars .... Marbled S.
      (d) Small bluish spots all over .... Jefferson's S.
      (e) Yellowish spots in two rows along back .... Spotted S.
   (2)   *Orange-red body,* on each side a row of red spots circled in black (land phase) .... Red newt
c. *Pond* salamanders,
   (1)   *Greenish body,* with a row of red spots, on each side; yellow beneath (water phase).................................. Red newt

B. *Toads*
  1.   Throat and belly spotted, dark spots on back usually contain single wart............American toad
  2.   Throat and belly not spotted, dark spots on back contain several warts .... Fowler's toad

C. *Frogs*
  1.   *Tree frogs. Adhesive disks on fingers and toes*
     a. 1 inch. Skin of back smooth, no white under eye .... Spring peeper
     b. 2 inch. Skin of back warty, white spot under eye .... Tree frog
  2.   *Frogs. Size larger, no disks on fingers and toes*
     a. *Large dark spots on back*
       (1)   Spots roundish, hind legs white below .... Leopard frog
       (2)   Spots squarish, hind legs yellow below ....Pickerel frog
     b. *No large spots on back*
       (1)   Grayish or reddish-brown, black mask .... Wood frog
       (2)   Greenish, back with dorso-lateral folds .... Green frog
       (3)   Greenish, back with *NO* dorso-lateral folds ....Bullfrog

GREEN FROG

DORSO-LATERAL FOLD

Reproduced by permission of MASSACHUSETTS AUDUBON SOCIETY, Lincoln, Massachusetts.

Figure 6–17   Adult Snakes of Massachusetts

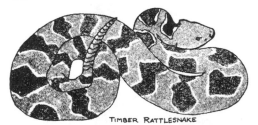

I. *Head oval, eye pupils round. Harmless snakes.*
    A. *Spotted or blotched with color*
        1. Grayish, with chestnut blotches above black rectangles beneath ....*Milk snake*
        2. Dark above, with reddish bands, whitish beneath, spotted red.................................... *Water snake*
        3. Grayish, with dark crosswise bands, upturned nose ....*Hog-nosed snake*
    B. *Striped snakes*
        1. Small size, slender, with three *thin* lengthwise bright yellow stripes ....*Ribbon snake*
        2. Larger size, stripes *pale* yellow
            .... *Garter snake*
    C. *Plain color*
        1. Green above, light color beneath
            .... *Smooth green snake*
        2. Black above
            a. Black below, white on chin, rounded cross section ○ ....*Black racer*
            b. Lighter below, chin white or cream, cross section like loaf of bread (Pilot Black) ◠ ....
                .... *Black rat snake*
        3. Metallic gray above, yellow beneath, neck collar
            .... *Ring-necked snake*
        4. Brownish above, bright red beneath (DeKay's)
            .... *Red-bellied snake*
        5. Brownish above, gray or pinkish beneath (DeKay's) .... *Northern brown snake*
II. *Head large and triangular, eye pupils elliptical. Poisonous.*
    A. Large size, copper-red above and below with dark crosswise bands above .... *Copperhead*
    B. Large size, two color phases—yellow with dark crosswise bands or dark with crosswise bands, tail with rattle of horny segments .... *Timber rattlesnake*

The triangular head and elliptical eye pupil are characteristic of poisonous snakes in Massachusetts. ◡ ◑
However in other parts of the country, other features are also important in identifying poisonous snakes. Learn to recognize the poisonous snakes of your community.

Reproduced by permission of MASSACHUSETTS AUDUBON SOCIETY, Lincoln, Massachusetts.
Artwork by Mary Shakespeare

ENVIRONMENTAL EDUCATION

Some snakes appear to give birth to live young because the eggs are retained inside the mother's body until maturity. Generally, reptiles lay eggs on land and cover them with soil to maintain good insulation and avoid temperature changes. Upon hatching some species of reptiles (sea turtles and snapping turtles) go immediately to the water and remain there except to lay eggs. Lizards spend their entire lives on land. Other amphibians like salamanders move back and forth from land to water according to their needs.

BIRDS Birds are warm-blooded animals with body temperatures that remain constant throughout the year. They have a coating of feathers that serve as a protection against winter cold. They have several different kinds of feathers, for example, down feathers that may be "fluffed up" in cold weather to create air pockets; contour feathers that cover the body; and flight feathers that are on the wings. Each year birds gradually drop their feathers and get new ones. Birds often have layers of fat to aid in insulating their small bodies.

Birds have a variety of distinguishing features that aid in their identification.

Figure 6–18
Bird Size

1. *Size* (Figure 6–18)   Three general size comparisons:

SPARROW 6 inches long

ROBIN 9 inches long

CROW 18 inches long

Train your eyes to judge bird size from several distances: close by, in a tree, while in flight.

Figure 6–19
Bird Shape

2. *Shape* (Figure 6–19)   What is the body shape—long–slender or short–stubby? Notice special features like the kind of tail, shape of feet, length of legs, appearance of wings.

Look carefully at the beak (Figure 6–20) to see how it is adapted to gathering certain kinds of food. Compare grosbeaks, finches, and sparrows-seed; warbler-insects; robins-worms; and gulls and terns-fish.

Figure 6–20
Bird Beak

Figure 6–21
Bird Crest

Is the bird crested (Figure 6–21) like a kingfisher, jay, cardinal, or titmouse?

3. *Behavior* How does the bird go about feeding? Does it scratch for insects on the ground like the towhee? Or peck at tree bark like the downy woodpecker? Or does it flip off bark in search of insects like the larger hairy woodpecker?

4. *Flight pattern* (Figure 6–22) The shape of a bird is important in flight. Does the bird soar? Travel on air currents? Does it have a fast or slow wing beat? Does it have long, slender wings to make swift, sharp turns like swallows and swifts, which can make sudden turns and catch insects while flying?

Figure 6–22   Flight Pattern

5. *Field marks* Does the bird have markings on its head, throat, breast, wings, or tail? Train yourself to recognize where the bird is darkest and lightest; striped or spotted, and so forth.

6. *Songs or calls* Many birds have more than one song and numerous call notes. Some of the songs are used to establish territory; some are for mating. Some are calls to sound alarms, summon for feeding, or call together a group. Songs or calls can be recognized by pitch, timing, loudness, phonetic likeness (e.g., chick-a-dee), quality, and tone.

7. *Habitats* A habitat must provide food, water, shelter, and, during nesting time, an increased amount of protection for the young. Female birds and the very young are often the same color as their surroundings. This camouflage protects them from prey and is often a clue for locating their habitat. A variety of different birds can be sighted on a border between two habitats. Large birds will nest in dense grass and thickets, while smaller birds will build nests off the ground in trees and tall shrubs.

Figure 6–23   Nests and Eggs

8. *Nests and eggs* (Figure 6–23)   Birds can be identified by their eggs and nest types. Eggs differ in size and color. Notice the height of the nest from the ground. Baltimore orioles build nests high in trees, sparrows in bushes or on the ground, and kildeer on the ground.

9. *Color, plus* (Figure 6–24)   Do not depend on color alone to remember a bird. Some colors can be deceptive. Red, yellow, and black show well. Most others do not. Light and reflection can change color shades, especially blue. Get plenty of other clues besides color, like field marks and size, what it was doing, and where it was located.

MAMMALS   Mammals vary in size and shape and are the most complicated of the vertebrates. Most mammals live on or in the land with the

Figure 6–24   Color, Plus

where was it ?

what was it doing ?

how does it fly ?

exception of bats, whales, dolphins, porpoises, seals, walruses, and manatees who either live in the air or in the water.

1. General characteristics
   a. Warm-blooded; internal control to maintain constant body temperature.
   b. Body covering of fur or hair to aid in keeping constant temperature. (Even people and whales have some body hair.)
   c. Produce milk to feed young, which are born alive, except for duck-billed platypus.
   d. A complete digestive and circulatory system. Breathe air with lungs, have four-chambered heart.
2. Food habits
   a. Herbivores eat plant material.
   b. Deer, cow, goat: grinding teeth predominate; canines and incisors of upper jaw replaced by horny pad used with lower incisors for cropping vegetation.
   c. Most rodents, porcupine, beaver, chipmunk, voles, woodchucks: long, self-sharpening teeth (enameled only on front, hence wear away unevenly to sharp edge); incisors for gnawing; no canines.
   d. Rabbits have doubled incisors in front, make neat diagonal cut on twigs and bark.
   e. Carnivores are meat-eating animals with strong jaws. They have sharp incisors and pointed canines for tearing meat. Premolars and molars are adapted for shearing rather than grinding. Examples are weasels, foxes, and cats.
   f. Omnivores are animals whose teeth are adapted for eating both plants and animals. Examples are the raccoon and opossum.
   g. Insectivores are animals whose small, sharp teeth are most efficient for a diet consisting mostly of insects. Examples are moles and shrews. Figure 6–25, Skullduggery Among the Mammals, shows how mammal's teeth have adapted for different food sources.
3. Adaptation to winter
   a. *Active* Squirrels, raccoons, and chipmunks usually are resting but may become active on sunny days.
   b. *Hibernating* In eastern woodlands; jumping mouse, brown bat, and woodchuck. All eat heavily in fall, store fat, life processes slow to a minimum.
   c. *Migrating* Mountain sheep and caribou migrate southward from the arctic tundra. Some bats migrate. Some humans go south.

Figure 6–25   Skullduggery Among the Mammals or Food Getting Adaptations

Tooth and jaw structure tell us so much about the eating habits of mammals that a good student can tell by the skull alone what animal it belongs to. Each species has its characteristic dentition ("arrangement of teeth," cf. "dentist"): combinations of the following:

INCISOR (cutting)   CANINE (tearing)   MOLAR (grinding)

The teeth of mammals are adapted in different ways to get food.

HERBIVOROUS

grinding molars
clipper-like incisors
no canines

Gnawers of seeds, roots, and stems. **Rodents**

Field mice and **woodchucks,** like all rodents, have long incisors, and a space between the incisors and molars. The chewing area can be closed off by a fold of skin for food storage.

Stem croppers. Ungulates ("having hoofs")

Cows and **deer** have no upper incisors. They tear grass with lower teeth and lips against the upper roof plate. **Sheep** and **goats** have similar dentition, but crop the grass closer as their jaws are narrower, and lips thinner. Sheep are not popular on cattle ranches!

Horses bite grass stems. They have both upper and lower front teeth.

INSECTIVOROUS

All teeth sharp-pointed, suitable for catching, holding and cutting prey.

Insect Eaters. Insectivores

Insects are attracted to plants of the fields and grasslands, and they, in turn, attract **moles** and **shrews.** These animals have a battery of small teeth useful in seizing and crunching hardshell beetles and other small fry.

CARNIVOROUS

sharp molars for tearing and cutting,
canines for slashing.

Meat Eaters. Carnivores

Field mice, moles, and shrews attract **foxes,** who feed on them and on rabbits, abundant in grassy meadows. Foxes have teeth equipped to handle meat. The canine teeth help seize and tear prey.

OMNIVOROUS

Such animals as **opossums, skunks, coons,** and **man** are omnivorous; literally eating anything. This broad diet is reflected in the teeth which are less specialized than in most mammals.

UPPER

2 INCISORS
1 CANINE
2 PRE-MOLARS
3 MOLARS

DENTAL FORMULA (MAN)

$\frac{2}{2} \frac{1}{1} \frac{2}{2} \frac{3}{3}$

3 MOLARS
2 PRE-MOLARS
1 CANINE
2 INCISORS

LOWER

Dentition is expressed in a dental formula. The example given means that in one-half of man's jaw, from front to back, there are 2 upper and 2 lower incisors, 1 upper and 1 lower canine, 2 upper and 2 lower pre-molars, and 3 upper and 3 lower molars.

Reproduced by permission of MASSACHUSETTS AUDUBON SOCIETY, Lincoln, Massachusetts.

ANIMAL ACTIVITIES

ARTHROPODS **Purpose** To focus attention on specific characteristics of arthropods that help the animals to meet their needs.

Equipment
Activity 1. Hand lens (optional).
Activity 7. Collecting containers.
Activities 8 and 9. Hand trowels.

Activities
1. Have students *locate an insect* and try to answer the following questions:
   a. How does it eat: by chewing (grasshopper)? siphoning (butterfly)? lapping (bee)? sponging (fly)? or piercing (sucking bugs)?
   b. How does it see? Are the eyes individual? Compound? How does it feel? Are there sensory organs (antennae) for detecting taste or odor?
   c. How does it travel? How many legs does it have? Are they long? Short? How does it use them? Are there claws on the feet?
2. Students can *turn over stones and logs* and see what lives beneath. Does the animal flinch from the light? Scurry to find darkness? How has it adapted to life in narrow cracks and under things? Is it round or flat?
3. Students can *locate a bee or ant nest* and observe what goes on. What are they doing? Could you establish an ant colony? A bee colony? What would be absolutely necessary? (A queen.)
4. Have each student *choose a different plant type*. Count and record the location and habits of the different insects on that plant. How do they adapt to the growth habits of the plant? For example, the milkweed plant attracts the monarch caterpillar, the milkweed bug, and a pink and white spider. The monarch caterpillar is hatched in 3 to 5 days from a pale green conical egg. The larvae feed on the leaves of the milkweed plant. They are well camouflaged and difficult to find. The pink and white spider sits in the pink and white flowers and waits for insects that come to the milkweed flower.
5. Ask students to *find different ways insects mimic the colors of the flowers or the patterns of bark*. Some stand rigid like twigs; some are the same color as flowers, trees, bark.
6. Take a short walk with students so they can try to *find at least five different insect homes* or signs of insect activity, for

example, cocoons, holes in the ground, borings in tree bark, eaten or rolled up leaves.

7. *Go on a gall hunt* with students. Galls are produced by the plant's response to an insect egg laid in the plant tissue. They are found on leaves, branches, twigs, and other plant surfaces. Students can open a fresh gall to see if they can find eggs or larvae inside. If not, a predator may have eaten them. Winter is a particularly good time to look for galls. Open just one. Leave some for nature. Fine some of the galls illustrated in Figure 6–26.

8. Students can *collect litter and soil* from a place that will be covered with water in spring. Have them place the contents in a dish of water and observe it for a few days. Mosquito larvae, fairy shrimps, and other exciting creatures may appear. They can use a hand lens to aid in studying the body structure of the animals. If the animals they collect use up all their food, have them give them some powdered cereal. Also, tell students to watch closely and see if animals eat each other.

9. Before the ground freezes in winter, students should *take a*

Figure 6–26   Galls

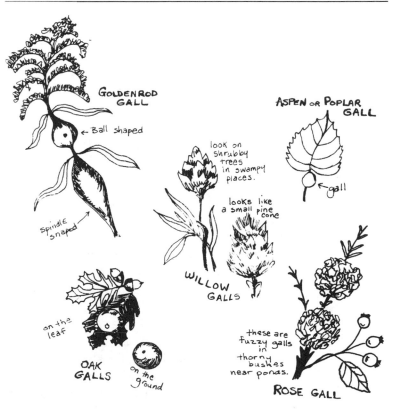

shovel full of soil indoors and warm it up. How many different living creatures come to life from each shovel full of earth? Students can look at them through a hand lens.

10. Winter is a good time for students to *look for insect life in and on the snow.* Snowfleas eat lichen and algae under the snow and can be seen hopping on top of the snow on warm winter days.

11. Ask students to *see how many signs of life can be found* in a place sheltered from the cold, such as a brick wall or the bark of a tree. There should be spider webs with egg cases; cocoons; resting mosquitoes or flies; woolly bear caterpillars that are waiting to pupate and emerge as moths in spring; centipedes, crickets, eggs; queen wasps waiting to start a new colony; and even ladybug beetles who will crawl into cracks and stay for the winter.

12. Tell students to *search through twigs and dead leaves* for insect eggs, cocoons, or other insect larvae.

Teacher Tips   This is an opportunity to promote respect for life and to guide students in the proper handling of insects to insure that they are not hurt and are cared for properly. When making observations of animals in their natural habitat, teach students not to poke hands or sticks into the animal's home. Relate the action to invasion of the children's homes.

BIRDS   **Purpose**   To learn identifying features of various birds.

Equipment
Activity 1.   Discarded container.
Activity 2.   Pot with soil.

Activities
1. With students, make simple bird feeders or bird homes that will attract a variety of birds using recycled materials as shown in Figure 6–27. Put out different kinds of seeds, breads, and doughnuts, and watch to see what each bird eats. Try some nuts and fruits.

2. Tell students to look for old birds' nests that have blown out of the trees. How many of the materials in the nest come from the immediate vicinity? They should separate twigs from the grass and other materials. Count how much of each material was used, and see what the bird preferred most. Ask if they can tell by the shape and size of the nest what birds lived there? Do they think there is any life in the nesting materials? Could insects be living in it? Have students put the nest in an

Figure 6-27 Recycling Is for the Birds

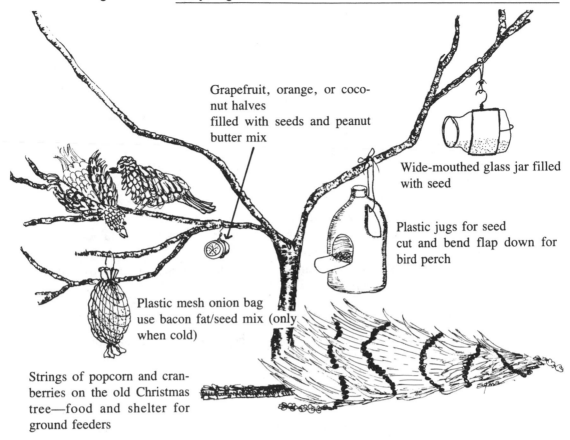

Grapefruit, orange, or coco-
nut halves
filled with seeds and peanut
butter mix

Wide-mouthed glass jar filled
with seed

Plastic jugs for seed
cut and bend flap down for
bird perch

Plastic mesh onion bag
use bacon fat/seed mix (only
when cold)

Strings of popcorn and cran-
berries on the old Christmas
tree—food and shelter for
ground feeders

enclosed area and observe it for a few days. Have them bury it
in soil and see if anything grows. Why are there seeds in a
nest?

3. Instruct students to look for holes in trees. Who might live in
these holes? (Squirrels, insects, racoons, chickadees, bats,
and so forth.) Have woodpeckers been drilling for food in the
tree or have they made a home there?

4. Tell students to pretend they are birds and have to keep warm.
They should wear something light, thick, and fluffy, like a
sweater or an insulated jacket, and something tightly woven to
keep out the wind. Birds have a layer of fluffy down feathers
underneath and a jacket of covering feathers on top. During
cold weather the body uses more fuel to keep warm, so a bird
(or you) must eat enough food to provide sufficient body
warmth. A sparrow needs twice as much food in winter as in
summer. Birds stand on one foot at a time, pulling the other up
under their feathers to keep it warm. Ask students if they have
ever been with only one glove and had to put their uncovered

hand under their jacket to keep it warm. Birds also tuck their bills under their feathers to breathe warm air under the rest of their body. Have the students ever pulled a scarf over their mouths and noses and done the same thing? Or breathed through their gloves?

Teacher Tips   The name of the bird is not important. What it was doing, its color, size, wing span, what it was eating, and its sounds are most important.

ANIMALS
(ESPECIALLY MAMMALS)

Purpose   To learn about mammals by observing their activities.

Equipment
Activity 2.   Yardstick.
Activity 3.   Plaster of Paris, water, mixing container, cardboard, and paraffin.
Activity 5.   Jars, cans, insulating materials, and thermometer.
Activity 6.   Plastic bags.

Activities
1.   *Animals tracks* may be traced in sand, soil, mud, and snow. Using Figure 6–28, A Beginner's Alphabet of Winter Tracks, and Figure 6–29, Basic Grammar of Track Language, students can do some detective work and see what they can find out about the animal. Was it running, walking, or hopping? Was it large like a fox or small like a bird? Did it drag its tail? How many animals were in the area?
2.   Have students *make tracks of their own* and see if anyone can tell how they were moving. Does the size of their foot and length of their leg determine their track? Tell them to measure the distance between a running footprint and a walking one.
3.   Teach students how to *prepare plaster casts of animal footprints* by encircling the print with a cardboard collar and filling the track with plaster of paris. (Plaster of paris may be purchased at any hardware store.) It should be mixed with water until it is the consistency of whipped cream. When the plaster is dry they will have a permanent print. This is more successful in mud than in snow. Use melted paraffin for prints in snow. Let the paraffin cool until the surface is covered with a skin before pouring onto the snow.
4.   Tell students to *look for signs of feeding*. Skunks make holes while searching for grubs. Squirrels leave piles of nut shells. They dig down through snow to the earth to find nuts. Birds and squirrels tear apart pine cones to get at the tiny seeds. Fungi and lichens grow on the sides of trees and rocks and are eaten by mice and squirrels. Rabbits, mice, and deer browse on the twigs of low shrubs and plants.

Figure 6–28 A Beginner's Alphabet of Winter Tracks & Signs

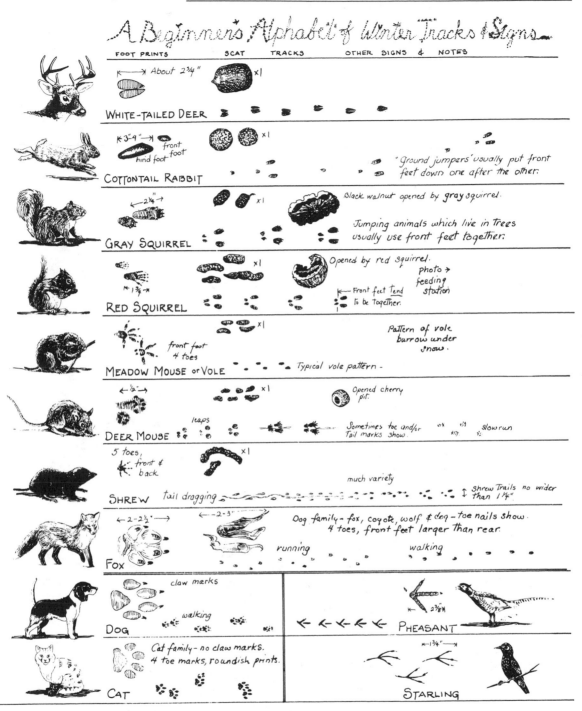

Artwork by Charles E. Roth and Mary S. Shakespeare

Remember: Tracks are variable and depend on the weather and ground conditions so use your head as well as your eyes and see what you can find. Reproduced by permission of MASSACHUSETTS AUDUBON SOCIETY, Lincoln, Massachusetts.

Figure 6–29 Basic Grammar of Track Language: The tracks of an animal can tell much about its life. Perhaps if you examine carefully all the tracks in a small area they will tell you a story. For instance

WHAT WAS THE ANIMAL DOING? WAS IT

RUNNING?   WALKING?

(foxes etc.)

DID IT CHANGE PACE?   OR SIT DOWN?   OR DRAG ITS TAIL?

(rabbit)

(deer mouse)

DID IT MAKE

A HOLLOW?   A HOLE?

A BURROW?

Where does it go?

Is it straight or curved?

Rabbits make small beds under grass or bushes.

Ruffed grouse burrow into snow in very cold weather.

Are there footprints or scat?

A YARD?
(deer)

Fox and deer make larger beds in grass.

DID IT LEAVE
WING MARKS?

without bird tracks

usually means bird taking off.

(pheasant or grouse)

usually mean an attack by hawk or owl. (P.S. Rabbit got away).

with bird tracks

TERRITORY MARKS?

Many animals mark their territory the way a dog does in passing a fire hydrant. Look for a hole in the snow with yellow stains around it, usually at the base of a tree, or on a snow hummock.

SCAT OR DROPPINGS?
Scat will help to identify an animal as well as what it ate.

Artwork by Mary S. Shakespeare and Charles E. Roth

5. *Mammals have fur to insulate them in winter*. A heavy fur coat in winter keeps animals warm just as it does for us. Many animals shed fur in warm weather to help cool their bodies. Removing our clothing in summer is much the same as animals shedding their fur. Students can experiment with jars or cans of water outdoors. Have them fill up several jars with boiling water and wrap each one in a different material. Try cotton, synthetics, wool, and fur. Take temperature readings every 10 minutes and see which temperature is dropping most rapidly. Why? Which material gives the best insulation?

6. Teach students to *identify some animals from their droppings*, called *scat*. Plastic bags are useful for collecting specimens, and a stick will come in handy if specimens are wet. Animal size, species, diet, and health may be determined by examining droppings. Rabbit and deer droppings are common and, therefore, easier to identify than many other types. Small animals like the grey squirrel and mice have a similar type of droppings but it is more difficult to find. Raccoon droppings can sometimes be identified by its location since the animal tends to deposit it on logs, limbs, and rocks. Members of the cat and dog family try to cover their droppings to hide their presence.

   Questions relevant to a study of droppings include: Is the animal a vegetarian? Look for berries, seeds, and grasses. Is it carnivorous? Look for hair, feathers, and undigested animal parts. Is it omniverous? Look for a variety of plant and animal parts.

   Students can look for seeds and insects in animal droppings. Why are they there? What will become of the droppings?

7. Ask students *how an owl pellet is different from droppings*. Owls eat small prey whole or tear large prey into chunks that they can swallow. After the animal has been digested, the remaining bones, hair, and feathers are coughed up as a pellet. Students can separate a pellet by soaking it in water overnight. Ambitious students may want to make a display of bones and hair from owl pellets or may try to reconstruct parts of one skeleton.

   If students cannot find a pellet, borrow one from a local naturalist to examine it.

Teacher Tips   These activities may be done at any time of the year. Signs that are more difficult to find in warm seasons may be easier to find in the snow in winter when animal homes, tracks, and feeding areas are more visible.

Water is a peculiar substance, even though one so familiar that we take it for granted. Among ordinary liquids it stands quite apart. Water must be drunk, or in some way taken into living bodies, because there is no life without it. Not only aquatic animals, but we and all animals and plants that have gotten away from water as a home are inevitably dependent on water.[3]

Robert E. Coker
Streams, Lakes, Ponds

WATER AND ITS INHABITANTS

In preparation for on-site water life study, stimulate student's curiosity by providing background material before going out. Ponds and lakes are discussed in this workshop. However, there are many other water habitats that can be studied such as swamps, marshes, bogs, oceans, rivers, and drainage ditches (see Figures 6–30, 6–31, 6–32, and 6–33).

Ponds and Lakes

What is the difference between a pond and a lake? *Ponds* are shallow enough for plants to grow all the way across the bottom. *Lakes* are so deep that light cannot reach the bottom in the deepest parts; therefore, plants *do not* grow all the way across.

What different types of plant and animal life can be found in

(Continued on page 113)

[3]Copyright 1954 The University of North Carolina Press. Reprinted by permission of the publisher. p. 30.

Figure 6-30 Pond

It is easy to guess the name of the *backswimmer* whose back is shaped like the bottom of a boat and whose legs serve as oars.

The *water boatman* can swim but often is found scavenging on the bottom. It is most active on dark days.

Look in the water for a *water scorpion.* It breathes through a tube at the rear of its body while feeding under water. Take a look at its sharp beak. This is a good weapon!

A *water strider* walks on water. It also has wings and can disappear from an aquarium!

Water spiders walk on water. How does a strider differ from a spider?

The *Whirligig beetle* is named for the way it moves along the water. It has long, slender front legs.

The *Leopard frog* feeds on the pond animals listed above. It needs to be kept wet, and it must be handled with care or its long legs will break.

Figure 6–31   Temporary Pond (A water hole that dries up in summer)

This *tadpole* is special and turns into a salamander. What do most tadpoles become?

A *tubiflex worm* is reddish colored. Its tail waves above its head, which is buried in the mud.

A short animal with a short name, is a *scud.* Watch how it travels.

A *copepod* is so tiny it can barely be seen without a hand lens. The bulging side pockets contain eggs.

Mosquito larvae, called "wigglers," are food for dragonflies and dragonfly larvae.

Even when the *dragonfly nymph* turns into an adult it continues to eat mosquitoes. We could use more dragonflies!

Damselfly nymphs feed on plant materials and are valuable food for fish. Some burrow in mud, cling to rocks, or are free swimming.

Water beetles are very hungry insects. They feed on any animal they can catch in the water, including small fish. Which pair of legs helps this beetle travel?

A *fairy shrimp* has a pink color and has legs that move in a wave motion. It may be clasping an egg case in its legs.

Draw a picture of something else you saw at the pond!

Figure 6—32   Marsh—Swamp

A *green frog* goes "chug-arund" and is a champion mosquito eater. Watch it catch some!

Plants, such as buttonbush and dogwood shrubs, and cattails and grasses are common.

The *muskrat* has a soft brown fur and a naked tail. Muskrat homes are holes in banks or domes made with cattails, which they also eat.

A *duck* nests on the ground in the swamp.

The *redwing blackbird* has red and sometimes yellow shoulders. It nests in the shrubs.

The *grackle* can be seen nesting in tall conifers along the edge of the swamp. It is all black with a long tail.

A *snake* swims between plants and can sometimes be seen hanging in the bushes.

What else can be found in the swamp or marsh?

Figure 6–33 River

The most common *algae* are in the form of green threads, which provide food and hiding places for many animals. Look at algae closely with a hand lens.

There are several kinds of *leeches* in different colors. Try to find some on the underside of rocks. How do they feel to you? What do you think they eat?

In the summer a whole river may be carpeted with these tiny *duck weed* plants. A pair of leaves floats on top and one or two roots hang below.

The *pond weed* plant is rooted on the bottom of the river. Even the flowers are below water. Pond weed provides nesting material and food for many animals, including ducks.

Almost everyone recognizes the *duck,* which is well camouflaged and difficult to find.

By waiting patiently and quietly, you may see a *sunfish* making a nest in warm, shallow water. What do they use to make their nest?

Watersnakes live in the water but they lay their eggs on land. They are not poisonous but if made angry, they will bite.

There are several kinds of *turtles* in a river. On warm days they will leave the water to lay *eggs* on land. It is possible to watch a turtle lay her eggs if you are very quiet and keep a distance.

Look for shelled *snails* and *clams* along the shore. What preys on them?

ENVIRONMENTAL EDUCATION

Figure 6–34   Cross Section of a Pond

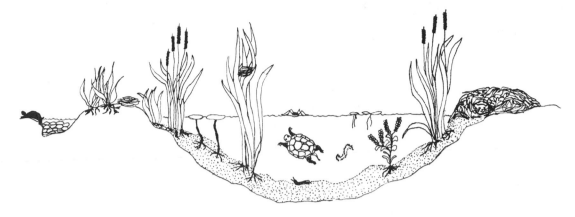

and around a pond or lake? See Figure 6–34, Cross Section of a Pond. Students should be encouraged to look for plants and animals in the water, on top of the water, and on the bottom of a pond. They can become acquainted with some water plants and animals before going out by making identification cards of plants and animals they expect to find. The cards can be put in plastic wrap to protect them from getting wet. Encourage students to concentrate on how an organism moves (if animal), where it lives in the water, and how it gets its food and oxygen. Observe how both plant and animal structures are modified to survive in the water.

It is difficult for the younger student to view a body of water as a single ecosystem. However, it is easy to look at particular habitats within a body of water. Habitats are the special places where groups of plants and animals live. For example, a cross section of a pond (Figure 6–34) reveals a surface habitat, a midwater habitat (below the surface and above the bottom), and a bottom habitat.

SURFACE LIFE   Most surface dwellers prey on one another or eat plants that are floating on the surface of the water. Some even depend upon eating drowned insects that are floating on the surface. Some small animals depend on the surface water tension to get around after their food. This is demonstrated each time a water strider or water spider "walks" across the water. There are also plants on the surface of the water. Some are floating freely while others, such as water lilies, are rooted in the bottom and only *look* as if they are floating on top.

MIDDLE LIFE   The middle level is a feeding ground for a variety of organisms. These organisms range in size from microscopic plants and animals, collectively known as *plankton,* to larger animals such as fish. Floating green plants in the form of algae, though difficult to see early in spring without a microscope, often become more obvious as summer approaches. Plankton, which vastly outnumber the larger organisms, are at the bottom of the food chain and serve as food for the larger organisms in the water. Some flying insects lay eggs in the water, and the larvae of these insects may be found feeding on the plankton of the middle layer. Some of these larvae stay in the middle layer while others only feed in the middle but live on the bottom. Larvae are, in turn, often eaten by larger organisms. All of the living plants and animals of the pond or lake are part of an intricate food chain.

In spring look for frog, toad, or salamander eggs in the middle layer. They appear as strings or masses of jellylike eggs and will hatch into tadpoles. Maturation of the tadpoles varies with the species, but it can be as long as 3 years. You may want to collect a few eggs to raise in an aquarium. Remember, overcrowding will cause everything to die! Directions for building and maintaining an aquarium are included in this chapter.

BOTTOM LIFE   The muddy territory of the bottom may look uninteresting, yet one shovel of bottom mud and a couple of rooted plants can produce many organisms for study. Crayfish, snails, clams, and caddisfly larvae are some of the animals found here. The caddisfly larvae often live under rock edges. They build a tube with bits and pieces of plants and sand cemented by saliva that they produce. The head and front legs may be seen sticking out of the tube as the animal eats algae. Two tail hooks hold them in the tube. In addition, nymphs of mayflies, damselflies, and dragonflies can sometimes be found burrowed in the muddy bottom.

SNAILS   Snails are favorites of many students and travel through all three habitats in a pond or lake. They may be found by turning over rocks in the water or on the underside of decaying leaves that are at the edge of a pond or lake. Snails can be collected for indoor study.

PHYSICAL CHANGES   Physical changes, which affect plant and animal life in the water, occur in ponds and lakes during the year. Oxygen is just as important to these plants and animals as it is to those of us who live on land. Fortunately for life in water, the highly oxygenated water at the surface circulates from top to bottom during a semiannual "turnover." This phenomenon is caused by the varying density of water at different temperatures. Water contracts and becomes more dense until it drops to 39.2°F, or 4°C. (Here is a chance for students to use the metric system.) Below this temperature it expands and gets lighter. At 32° it becomes ice, and floats because it is then lighter than an equivalent volume of water. In the fall as the water gets colder, it sinks until the bottom layer is 39°F. As the colder water sinks, warmer water is pushed up from below until the whole pond is 39°F and the fall "turnover" stops. It is then that surface water will get colder, expand and become lighter, and freeze into ice.

In the spring, the melting ice water warms up from 32°F to 39°F. As it gets to 39°F, it is denser than the water below, and this cold highly oxygenated water sinks and pushes the warmer water from below to the top. The spring "turnover" continues until the surface water is no longer colder than the water below. Thus the oxygen supply to the plants and animals at all levels of the water is renewed.

WATER ACTIVITIES

BUILDING AN AQUARIUM **Purpose** To duplicate a balanced natural system.

Equipment Large glass container filled almost to the top with water from the site, *not* the tap; sand and gravel for the bottom; a small piece of charcoal to filter out impurities.

Activity Have students make a balanced aquarium in a tank that has a capacity of six or more gallons. (A small, temporary aquarium can be made using large peanut butter jars and cafeteria mayonnaise jars, as shown in Figure 6–35, Homemade Aquarium.) It will take some experimenting before a balance between plant and animal life is achieved. This is part of the learning process.

1. To fill the aquarium, students put a piece of paper over the sand on the bottom of the aquarium and gently pour the water on top. The paper will prevent the sand from getting stirred up. They can remove the paper when the aquarium is full.
2. Natural plants from the body of water from which the specimens are collected are best for the aquarium. However, if students are not able to obtain any plants, they can try to find some of the following plants at the local aquarium store: *Vallisneria* (tape grass), *Sagittaria* (arrowhead), *Elodea* and *Myriophyllum*.
3. Some interesting creatures for the aquarium might be dragonfly larvae, daphnea, cyclops, or water striders. Tell students to watch to see which ones multiply, which preys on which,

Figure 6–35 Homemade Aquarium

how they get about the aquarium, and so forth. If the water gets cloudy, students can remove some of the plants. This cloudiness will indicate that the aquarium is not balanced. You may also try adding snails or tadpoles.

Teacher Tips

1. Above all, teach *respect* for life. Students must understand how important it is to provide for the needs of all organisms collected. All specimens studied should be returned to the water.

2. If it is not possible to provide a balanced system for the specimens, do not bring them indoors.

3. Aquariums should be kept in indirect light and away from heat sources (such as radiators).

4. A cover will prevent water evaporation and will prevent specimens from flying or jumping out.

5. Always replenish the water for an aquarium from the original site from which the specimens were collected. This water will

contain microscopic plants and animals for the larger aquarium animals to feed upon.

6. Several *Golden Guides* are useful at the site. (e.g., Reid, George K. *Pond Life. Golden Nature Guide.* New York: Golden Press, 1967).

GENERAL ACTIVITIES **Purpose** To study water habitats.

Equipment

Activity 1. Yardstick, thermometer.
Activity 2. Large jars to carry water and specimens indoors for study.
Activity 3. A white bleach or milk container cut out for scooping, as shown in Figure 6–36.
Activity 4. Small white container.
Activity 5. Yardstick, scissors, hand lens.
Activity 6. Container, water from habitat, magnifying glass.
Activity 7. Container, rocks, leaves, soil, and small amount of water.
Activity 8. Hammer, stake.
Activity 9. Yardstick, plaster of paris.
Activity 10. Hammer, chisel, container.

Activities:

1. In spring, have students *keep track of melting pond or lake water* and record when "turnover" begins. They can take a yardstick with a thermometer taped or screwed onto the stick and record surface temperatures. They should move the thermometer to the end of the yardstick and take another reading. Students keep recordings of temperature changes each week. These readings should tell them when the water at the bottom has finished "turning over."

2. *Look for toad or frog eggs.* In May the mother toad lays eggs in long jellylike strings along the edge of ponds and streams. (Frogs' eggs appear in gobs or masses.) Toad eggs will break out of their jelly in 4 or 5 days. If they are to be taken indoors for study, tell students to take only a few eggs. A very large aquarium will support only two or three tadpoles. Toads will not fully mature until mid or late summer so students should

Figure 6–36 Handmade Scoop

not take them back to a classroom unless they plan to release them before school ends.

3. Tell students to *scoop up a little surface water* and examine it very closely for life. It takes the eye a few minutes to see anything move. White provides a good contrasting background for this. Have each student choose a particular surface dweller to observe, and try to imitate its movements.

4. Have students *look for animals just below the surface of the water*. These are animals that get their oxygen from the surface, such as beetle larva, backswimmer, water boatman, giant water bug, diving beetle. Make sure they notice the silvery "bubble" of air at the tail end or all over the ventral surface of those who carry the air with them.

5. Instruct students to *measure the stem of a cattail* and see how tall it must grow to keep its head above water. Students can gently cut the cattail and bring the stem inside to examine it. What type of a stem does it have? Students should look at a cross section of the stem under the microscope or with a hand lens.

6. *Snails may be found in the water under rocks and leaves.* They may be kept indoors in water taken from their natural habitat. Place a container in fairly strong light to stimulate algae growth, but do not place it in the sun where heat will rob the water of oxygen. Snails crawl on a thick muscular "foot" on the underside of their bodies. A distinct head with two pairs of sensory tentacles can be extended or contracted (see Figure 6–37). A rasping tongue moves back and forth like a file against the wall of the tank gathering food in the form of algae. This is why snails are often included in aquariums. The jellylike masses that appear on the sides of the glass are snail eggs that will hatch to produce more snails.

Figure 6–37   Snail

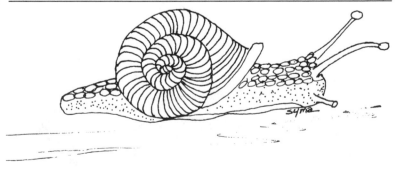

Put a magnifying glass up to the side of the aquarium so students can watch the snails eat. Would they be welcome in an algae-filled aquarium?

7. *Students can find planaria on the bottom of rocks* or catch them by leaving a piece of fresh liver in the water for an hour. (You will also collect leeches this way.) Planaria are flatworms, and they represent one type of invertebrate. They may be kept in a container and fed liver once a week. The liver must be removed when the animals leave it. The container should have rocks for them to crawl under and should be kept in a very dark corner of the room.

8. *Drive a stake into the ground* at the edge of the water. Students can check it each week, and add a stake when the water's edge has changed. Is the water receding? Rising? Is the variation predictable? What affects the water's level? Rain? Heat? Students keep track of air temperature and rainfall. They make a graph of the changes. These recordings can be useful in math studies.

9. *Measure a small section of a pond* 3 feet from the water's edge. Use a wooden yardstick. Tell students to describe everything that falls inside that yard including anything or anyone (bird) overhead. Repeat this weekly. Are there plants or animals that invade an area that was brown or dead looking the previous week? Have students make a list of the birds who live near the water and some of the reasons why. Are there plants that like to spend portions of their life in water but will be happy high and dry all summer? How do water grasses differ from meadow grasses? The students can take one of each apart and compare them. They should list all the larger animals that come to the water's edge. Why do they come? How can they tell they were there? (Footprints, droppings.) Students can make some plaster of paris casts of footprints in the mud (as described in Animal Life Activities).

10. With the students go to a pond, river, or stream in winter and *cut a hole in the ice*. Bring a sample of water and ice indoors and examine the variety of life in the water. As the ice melts, what else appears? How does this compare to a summer sample of water? Where do the plants and animals go in winter? Amphibians and some reptiles burrow into the mud beneath the water and remain quiet for the winter. Insects change in a variety of stages, each one adapted to maximum survival: that is larva, pupa, or adult. Seeds have protective covers, and roots and seeds survive in mud. Why is there more variety of life in summer?

Teacher Tips

1. Water life is easier to observe on a white background. Scoopers, specimen containers for small animals, and basins should be white plastic or white enamel.
2. For young students, plastic wrap stretched across a cylinder (tall juice can) can be used to view underwater activity.
3. A hand lens is useful for viewing larger water animals. Younger students need to practice focusing a hand lens before they go outdoors.
4. A 40× microscope with a dip slide can be fun for older students (above grade 4) to view microscopic organisms.
5. Students should be told to wear old clothes and old footwear. There is always mud or slippery plants around water, and accidents usually occur. Sneakers, which dry out fast, are good in summer, and rubber boots are good for other times of the year.
6. It is best to break larger groups into teams.
7. Students should be assigned specific water equipment for which they are responsible.

Follow-Up

1. *Make an ice cube using food coloring.* Lower it very gently into a glass of warm water. You will notice that while the ice floats the cold water melting from the cube sinks.
2. *Weigh a cup of cold water and a cup of hot water.* Is there a difference? This requires a sensitive scale. Try balancing one against the other if your scale is not sensitive enough.
3. *Get a shallow basin of warm water* and have one of the students take off his or her shoes and socks. Have the student stand in the water while you pour in a quart of very cold water. Where does he or she feel the cold water first? Ask the students to do this during bath time in their tubs at home.
4. *Put a freshly cut stalk of celery* into a jar containing five or six drops of colored water. (If the celery is cut too soon the tubes will seal.) Overnight the dye travels up the stem into the leaves. Look at the end of the stalk and see the "channels" appearing like colored dots. How does the celery stalk compare to the stem of a lily or cattail? To a pond grass or highland grass?

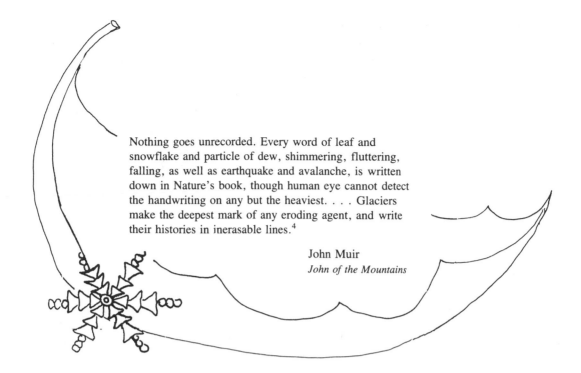

Nothing goes unrecorded. Every word of leaf and
snowflake and particle of dew, shimmering, fluttering,
falling, as well as earthquake and avalanche, is written
down in Nature's book, though human eye cannot detect
the handwriting on any but the heaviest. . . . Glaciers
make the deepest mark of any eroding agent, and write
their histories in inerasable lines.[4]

John Muir
John of the Mountains

PHYSICAL ENVIRONMENT

For hundreds of millions of years, the Earth's appearance has been
changing because of climate and Earth dynamics. Through repeat-
ed cycles of *uplift* (mountain building and folding) and *erosion*
(stream building and sedimentation), through water, wind, and
ice, the physical structure of the Earth has been altered. Recently,
human activities have brought about equally far-reaching physical
changes to the land, air, and water.

Structure of the Earth's Crust

The basic structure of the Earth's crust consists of rock formations
exposed at the surface as *bedrock*. Rocks are made up of one or
more minerals in three general categories: igneous, sedimentary,
and metamorphic. Like living organisms, rocks may be recycled

---

[4]Edited by Linnie Marsh Wolfe. Copyright, 1938, by Wanda Muir Hanna, page 88.
Copyright © renewed 1966 by John Muir Hanna and Ralph Eugene Wolfe. Reprinted by
permission of Houghton Mifflin Company.

and changed from one form to another. The hardest type of rock, and slowest to erode, is *igneous*—molten material that cooled and crystallized within the Earth's crust (granite) or at its surface (volcanic). *Sedimentary* rock usually erodes quite easily because it is composed of layers of sediments (sandstone, limestone, conglomerate) cemented together. *Metamorphic* rock can be igneous, sedimentary, or other metamorphic rock (marble, quartzite, gneiss) that has undergone change by heat and/or pressure. The kind of rock greatly influences the type of landform, such as valley or highland, visible to the human eye.

Glacial Periods

The most recent imprint in "Nature's book" was written during the glacial periods, which began about 1 million years ago. Climate changes caused layers of snow to accumulate at the North Pole forming an ice cap that began to move by its own weight. As it moved in a southeasterly direction, it scraped and gouged out everything in its path and left piles of debris. Four intervals of the advance and retreat of the glacier affected parts of the United States. Only 10 to 15,000 years ago the last glacier covered the northeastern portion of the United States as well as parts of the northern Midwest.

Landforms

Landforms created by the glacial periods, especially the last, remain to be examined. Boulders, which were chipped off bedrock hills and strewn about, are called *erratics*. *Glacial till* (small rocks and clay) was dragged along by ice, and this unsorted rubble was deposited as *ground moraine*. *Terminal moraines,* which formed at the southern edge of a stagnant glacier, created new areas such as Cape Cod and Long Island. Glacial till carried by the moving ice also was dumped as *drumlins,* or low hills with steep sides toward the direction from which the ice advanced. These smooth, elliptical hills dot much of the landscape of the northern United States today, although many have been mined for their gravel.

The melting glacier left behind *outwash plains* in front of the ice sheet and long, narrow, winding ridges of sand and gravel called *eskers*. Eskers were deposited by streams flowing under the ice or in ice cracks. Blocks of ice left behind formed depressions or *kettleholes* when the ice melted and glacial debris fell in. Often these depressions are quite deep and filled with water, such as

Walden Pond in Lincoln, Massachusetts, made famous by Henry David Thoreau.

Forces of Weathering

In addition to the landforms created by glaciation, the forces of weathering continue to change the shape of the land. Rocks are worn down by surface water, by the organic acids of decaying plants and animals on their surface, by wind sand-blasting their surfaces, and by water freezing in crevices and expanding to cause fractures. At the same time, running water from streams and rivers carves deep valleys in the land. The sediments carried downstream are deposited when the flow gradually decreases as it enters a larger body of water. This landform is called a *delta*. One of the largest deltas is at the mouth of the Mississippi River in Louisiana where the river enters the Gulf of Mexico.

Geologists can tell how sediments have been formed by their physical characteristics. Fast moving water that is tumbling down steep grades will deposit large and small particles along its course, whereas a smoothly flowing stream will drop out the larger rocks first and carry the finer particles further downstream.

Non-Renewable Resources

Knowledge of geology has enabled people to locate sources of underground fuel. Within the rock layers of the Earth, people found fuels (petroleum, gas, peat, and coal) with which to meet their energy needs. Petroleum and natural gas are believed to come from decayed marine plants and animals on the ocean floor. This organic material, buried under sediments, decayed without the presence of much oxygen. Through periods of pressure and heat it transformed into either liquid or gaseous hydrocarbon compounds. Natural gas and oil may be found under the ocean, or under the land where it has escaped through porous beds into pools. Coal and peat come from partly decayed vegetable matter and are generally found in old swamp beds. Coal was formed largely in the Carboniferous Period some 350 million years ago. Petroleum and gas are found in Cenozoic and Mesozoic rocks that were created 70 to 135 million years ago. These resources are *not renewable*.

In recent years petroleum and natural gas resources have begun to approach depletion. Coal is still one of industry's more plentiful fuels. It contains more carbon than oil or gas and, therefore, releases more carbon dioxide. However, scientists feel there is a way to prevent the release of carbon dioxide during the burning process. The noxious gases and particles that form smoke and enter the atmosphere can be eliminated, at great expense.

Air

The supply of air is also *not renewable*. Therefore, when the composition of the atmosphere is changed, long-term effects will occur. The atmosphere by volume is 78 percent nitrogen, 21 percent oxygen, 0.9 percent argon, and 0.03 percent carbon dioxide, plus traces of other gases and variable amounts of water depending upon the region.

CARBON DIOXIDE   Since 1860 the amount of carbon dioxide in the atmosphere has increased by 18 percent. Scientists claim that at the present rate of increase (caused by the burning of fossil fuels), the concentration of carbon dioxide in the atmosphere will increase more by the end of this century.

Accumulations of carbon dioxide in the atmosphere act like a greenhouse. Carbon dioxide lets sunlight hit the Earth but absorbs some of the heat and prevents it from radiating out into space. Green plants, forests, and oceans need carbon dioxide for photosynthesis, but their ability to absorb it is limited. Thus, carbon dioxide accumulates in the atmosphere, raising the Earth's temperature.

POLLUTION   In the process of industrialization, many countries of the world have contributed to the contamination of our atmosphere by adding gases and chemicals from industrial waste. Rains and snows, which fall on the land, are later returned to the oceans through flowing rivers and streams. Water again evaporates from the oceans, rivers, lakes, and streams and once again is returned to the atmosphere. This continuous cycling of air and water has dispersed pollutants around the world. Sulfur oxides have eroded buildings and statues, and the acidity of water supplies has been increased.

Changing Environment

It is not enough today to understand only ecological balances within plant and animal communities. More must be learned about how these communities depend upon the physical environment and how that environment is changing.

The challenge is to learn to use Nature's forces, such as sun, wind, water movement, and geothermal power. These sources will not run out. They are *renewable energy* sources. A good basic understanding of the physical environment will help citizens make intelligent choices in the future.

PHYSICAL ENVIRONMENT ACTIVITIES

Purpose   To examine the effects of pollution, weathering, erosion, and various geological processes on the land. To explore renewable and nonrenewable energy sources.

Equipment

Activity 4.	Shovel; sun reflector.
Activity 5.	White filter paper used for coffee pots.
Activity 6.	Clay pot with soil.
Activity 7.	Hand lens, black paper or cloth.
Activity 8.	Thermometer.
Activity 9.	Covered boxes.
Activity 10.	Colored paper.
Activity 11.	Twelve sticks.
Activity 14.	Two pans of water.
Activity 15.	Wind vain.
Activity 16.	Metal sheets, insulating material, thermometer, food.

Activities   Geological processes can be studied in winter using snow and ice as a substitute for soil and rock because snow may be manipulated and observed so easily.

1. *Students can be detectives to find out how the land was formed.* Geologists look at landforms to determine what came before. Ask some of the following questions: Was this valley once the riverbed of a giant glacier? Was this plain created by a glacier moving over a mountain top and shearing it off? Was this soil deposited by a melting glacier? Was this sand, rock, and soil rubbed from the side of a mountain by a grinding glacier? by a rushing stream?
2. *Students look for signs in the snow* that indicate how the land is used other times of the year. For example, snow will settle into the pattern of furrowed farm land; it will melt over a leaching field where human waste gives off energy in the process of decay; it will be "fluffed up" and uneven on grass

Figure 6–38
Snow Gauge

Make a snow gauge

where there are air spaces but will compact on concrete and other solid surfaces; and it will drift away from areas exposed to strong winds. Have students make a snow gauge and compare accumulated snow on the landscape to that in the gauge. (See Figure 6–38.)

3. *Students can build a snow (or mud) dam and observe it.* What happens to the space created when snow (or dirt) is removed from the land to make the dam? The wind may blow more snow (or dirt) into the space, water may come to fill it up, or other debris may catch in the hole. What will happen to the dam itself over a period of time? Rain may eventually erode it; wind may blow it down; or plants may grow in the soil. The land is constantly being changed by natural forces like wind, rain, and emerging plants.

4. *Students should make a clean cut in a snow bank,* and see if they can read the history of just one winter. Count the number of snowfalls by the change in texture from top to bottom. Snow can be transformed by compacting and compressing it, as when a snow ball is formed. Have them try squeezing a snow ball 30 seconds, 60 seconds, 90 seconds, and cutting it in half each time to see if there is a difference. Metamorphic rock is formed in much the same way through thousands of years of accumulated layers of rock that are compressed and changed by the pressure from above. This change can be seen in the layers of snow from several snowstorms. The layer on the bottom will almost be a solid mass of crystals. Proceeding up through the snow cut, each layer will be less and less compressed. At the top the snow will contain the greatest amount of air, and there will be a separation among the crystals. Heat also creates metamorphic rock, and this process can be duplicated by melting snow very slightly with a sun reflector.

Figure 6–39   Snow Filter

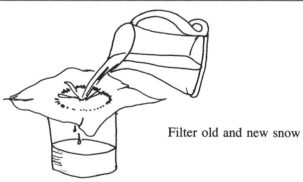

Filter old and new snow

5. *Tell students to filter snow,* as shown in Figure 6–39, to see what it contains. There is a dark line between layers of old snow. What caused the dark line? Is the filtered material natural, man-made, or a combination? This can be a very graphic pollution study.

6. *Students should place a clay pot full of soil* outdoors in winter and observe what happens. The soil freezes inside the pot, and the water in the soil expands until the pot bursts. This process can be seen in winter when roads form pot holes.

7. *The study of snow crystals* can be done with a hand lens outdoors. Students should observe crystals on a piece of frozen black cloth or on a piece of black paper. They can capture snowflakes and create permanent impressions on glass slides. Figure 6–40 gives directions, as well as shapes and classifications of snowflakes. A good follow-up activity is to fold paper and make cutouts of six-pointed snowflakes.

Figure 6–40   Preserving Snowflakes[5]

EQUIPMENT   clear lacquer spray
             glass microscope slides
             cardboard
             freezer

PROCEDURE

1. Store the lacquer spray can and several glass microscope slides in the freezer. Rest the slides on a piece of cardboard so heat from the hand will not warm them as they are removed from the freezer.

2. On a snowy day, quickly remove the can of lacquer and microscope slides from the freezer and take them out doors in a protected spot where they will stay cold but will not pick up falling snow.

3. Spray each slide with a thin coat of lacquer and place it in the falling snow.

4. When there are several snowflakes on each slide, remove the slide to where it will remain cold but be protected from additional snowfall. Allow the slides to dry for about one hour.

5. Bring the slides indoors. The lacquer will have preserved permanent impressions of a variety of snowflakes on the slides.

(continued)

---

[5]From *Field Guide to Snow Crystals* by Edward R. LaChapelle. Seattle, Wash.: University of Washington Press, 1969, p 11. Reprinted by permission.

Figure 6–40 *(continued)*

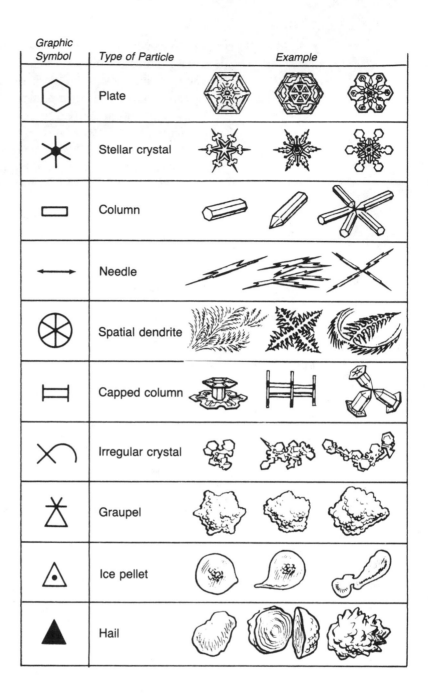

Graphic Symbol	Type of Particle	Example
⬡	Plate	
✳	Stellar crystal	
▭	Column	
↔	Needle	
⊕	Spatial dendrite	
⊟	Capped column	
⟨◠	Irregular crystal	
⟁	Graupel	
△	Ice pellet	
▲	Hail	

8. *Have students study temperature changes in a snow hole* as illustrated in Figure 6–41 by recording temperatures at various levels. Use a large meat-type thermometer that has a large dial that can be viewed from the surface. Because snow acts as an insulator, ground temperature should be warmer than surface temperature. They can compare temperatures

Figure 6–41   Temperature Study

part way into the snow bank. If the ground is too hard to get a thermometer into, rest it on the ground surface. This is a good time to discuss the importance of snow cover as insulation to plants and animals in winter.

9. *Have students prepare boxes with a door* for taking temperature readings. The door in the box should be large enough to insert a hand. They should put the boxes in two different places. For example, rest one in a field and one next to a building. Leave one exposed and cover the other. Students take temperature readings in the boxes at various times of the day for 1 week.

10. *Students can examine the effect color has* on absorbing or reflecting the sun's rays. Dark colors absorb, and light colors reflect. Thus, a white flag pole should have more snow at its base than an ordinary tree. Tell students to put a piece of black and a piece of white paper (or can lids of various colors) on the top of the snow and see what happens after several hours in the sun. As the black paper sinks into the snow and makes a depression, it will be evident how much of the sun's energy, which has melted the snow beneath, the black paper has absorbed. Does the whiteness of snow aid in

Figure 6–42
Sun Clock

reflecting the sun's rays in winter? How does that affect living things?

11. *Pick a sunny day and have students find a young sapling* that is out in the open. Have students place a stick in the snow, or if it is summer, in the soil, at the very end of the shadow. Every hour they should place another stick at the end of the shadow, as shown in Figure 6–42. If the first stick is inserted at 9:00 A.M., then one stick means it is 9 o'clock, 2 sticks means it is 10 o'clock, and so forth. Students can tell the time by shadow sticks the next day that it is sunny. Ask them where the sun was each hour? Why do shadows change in length and direction during the day? Are the shadows affected by seasonal change?

12. *Tell students to make a list of the types of fuels* used at home, at school, and in the community. Determine the source of these fuels and their cost by interviewing school committee members, town conservation officials, and state and federal employees.

13. *Have students make a list of the renewable resources* used in their community or state. Do they produce efficient and reliable sources of energy? Do they create additional problems?

14. *Instruct students to place two pans of water out in the sun.* Have them do nothing to one pan, but surround the other with aluminum foil to reflect sunlight into the pan. Does the latter pan of water heat up faster? How long does it take to heat the same quantity of water in the other pan? What potential energy source is created by hot water? Steam engines are turned by steam, which is created from boiling water. There are also sources of hot water within the Earth's crust. These are called *geothermal energy sources,* and in Greenland whole cities are heated by this hot water, which is taken out of the ground and piped directly into homes.

15. With class, purchase or *make a small windvane* and place it outside. Have students observe how often the windvane is moving. Is this a potential energy source? Is the windvane moving on a warm day when there appears to be no wind at all? Tell students to try to discover why the windvane is almost constantly in motion. (Rising heat is also an energy source.)

16. *With class build a solar oven* using metal reflectors and insulation material. Bake or heat foods in the oven to see how hot the oven will get. Use a thermometer to monitor temperature.

Teacher Tips   For winter activities, always remind students to dress warmly. Two lighter layers are warmer than one heavy layer.

Hats and mittens or gloves are vital. Relate human preparation for winter to the rest of the animal world. Make frequent but brief trips out in winter.

REFERENCES

Plants

CHILDREN   Anderson, Margaret. *Exploring City Trees and the Need for Urban Forests*. New York: McGraw-Hill, 1976.

Cowle, Jerry. *Discover the Trees*. New York: Sterling Press, 1977.

Dowden, Anne Ophelia. *Wild Green Things in the City*. New York: Thomas Y. Crowell, 1972.

————. *The Blossom on the Bough:* A Book of Trees. New York: Time–Life, 1975.

Edwards, Joan. *Caring for Trees on City Streets*. New York. Charles Scribner's Sons, 1975.

Jaspersohn, William. *How the Forest Grew*. New York: Greenwillow, 1980.

Lerner, Carol. *Flowers of a Woodland Spring*. New York: William Morrow, 1979.

List, Albert, Jr., and Ilka List. *A Walk in the Forest: The Woodlands of North America*. New York: Thomas Y. Crowell, 1977.

Rahn, Joan Elma. *Nature in City Plants*. Chicago, Ill.: Childrens Press, 1977.

————. *Watch it Grow/Watch it Change*. New York: Atheneum, 1978.

Selsam, Millicent. *Play with Plants*. New York: William Morrow, 1978.

Zim, Herbert S. *Plants: A Guide to Plant Hobbies*. New York: Harcourt Brace Jovanovich, 1947.

ADULTS   Brockman, Frank C. *Trees of North America*. New York: Golden Press, 1968.

Caras, Roger. *The Forest*. Boston: Houghton-Mifflin, 1979.

Elias, Thomas. *The Complete Trees of North America. Field Guide and Natural History*. An Outdoor/Life Nature Book. New York: Van Nostrand Reinhold, 1980.

Farb, Peter, and the editors of Time–Life. *The Forest*. New York: Time-Inc., 1961.

Harlow, William M. *Trees of the Eastern and Central United States and Canada*. New York: Dover, 1957.

Went, Frits W., and the editors of Time–Life. *The Plants*. New York: Time-Inc., 1963.

Plants: Wild Foods

CHILDREN   Hays, Wilma, and R. Vernon Hays. *Foods the Indians Gave Us. How to Plant, Harvest, and Cook the Natural Indian Way*. New York: David McKay, 1973.

Pringle, Laurence. *Wild Plants*. New York: Thomas Y. Crowell, 1975.
————. *Wild Foods: A Beginners Guide to Identifying. Harvesting and Preparing Safe and Tasty Plants from the Outdoors*. New York: Four Winds Press, 1978.

ADULTS Gibbons, Euell. *Stalking the Wild Asparagus*. New York: David McKay, 1970.
————. 1972. *Stalking the Healthful Herbs*.
Kavasch, Barrie. *Native Harvests. Recipes and Botanicals of the American Indian*. New York: Vintage Books, 1979.
Russell, Helen R. *Foraging for Dinner: Collecting and Cooking Wild Foods*. New York: Elsevier/Nelson Books, 1975.

Animal: Arthropod

CHILDREN Cole, Joanna, and Jerome Wexler. *Find the Hidden Insect*. New York: William Morrow, 1979.
Conklin, Gladys. *Praying Mantis: the Garden Dinosaur*. New York: Holiday House, 1978.
Mitchell, Robert, and Herbert S. Zim. *Butterflies and Moths*. Golden Guide Series. New York: Golden Press, 1964.
Patent, Dorothy Hinshaw, and Paul S. Schroeder. *Beetles and How They Live*. New York: Holiday House, 1978.
————. 1979. *Butterflies and Moths and How They Function*.
Selsam, Millicent E., and Joyce Hunt. *A First Look at Animals Without Backbones*. New York: Walker, 1976.
Van Soelen, Philip. *Cricket in the Grass*. New York: Charles Scribner's Sons, 1979.
White, William, Jr., and Sara Jane White. *A Mosquito is Born*. New York: Sterling Press, 1978.
Zim, Herbert S., and Clarence Cottam. *Insects: A Guide to Familiar American Insects*. Golden Guide Series. New York: Golden Press, 1951.

ADULTS Borror, Donald J., and Richard E. White. *A Field Guide to the Insects of America North of Mexico*. Boston, Mass.: Houghton-Mifflin, 1970
Brues, Charles T. *Insects, Food and Ecology*. New York: Dover, 1972.
Farb, Peter, and the editors of Life. *The Insects*. New York: Time-Inc., 1962.

Animals: Birds

CHILDREN Calahan, Philip S. *Birds and How They Function*. New York: Holiday House, 1979.
Drennan, Susan, ed. *Birder's Field Notebook*. New York: Doubleday, 1979.

Earle, Olive L. *Birds and Their Nests*. New York: William Morrow, 1952.

Farrar, Richard. *The Bird's Woodland: What Lives There*. New York: Coward, McCann & Geoghegan, 1976.

Flanagan, Geraldine Lux, and Sean Morris. *Window into a Nest*. Boston, Mass.: Houghton-Mifflin, 1976.

Hicks, J.L. *A Closer Look at Birds*. New York: Franklin Watts, 1976.

Peterson, Roger T. *How to Know the Birds*. New York: New American Library, 1971.

———. *The Birds*. Young Readers Library. New York: Silver Burdett, 1977.

ADULTS   Peterson, Roger Tory. *A Field Guide to the Birds*. Boston, Mass.: Houghton-Mifflin, 1963.

———. and the editors of Life. *The Birds*. New York: Time-Inc., 1963.

Reed, Chester A. *North American Birds Eggs*. New York: Dover, 1965.

Animals: Mammals

CHILDREN   Bancroft, Henrietta, and Richard G. VanGelder. *Animals in Winter*. New York: Thomas Y. Crowell, 1963.

Buck, Margaret Waring. *Where they Go in Winter*. New York: Abingdon Press, 1968.

Eimerl, Sarel, and Irven DeVore. *The Primates*. Young Readers Library. New York: Silver Burdett, 1977.

Karstad, Aleta. *Wild Habitats*. New York: Charles Scribner's Sons, 1979.

Milne, Lorus, and Margery Milne. *Gadabouts and Stick-at-Homes: Wild Animals and their Habitats*. New York: Charles Scribner's Sons/ Sierra Club Books, 1980.

Nussbaum, Hedda. *Animals Build Amazing Homes*. New York: Random House, 1979.

Patent, Dorothy Hinshaw. *Sizes and Shapes in Nature—What they Mean*. New York: Holiday House, 1979.

Selsam, Millicent. *How Animals Live Together*. New York: William Morrow, 1979.

Snedigar, Robert. *Our Small Native Animals: Their Habits and Care*. New York: Dover, 1963.

Weber, William J. *Care of Uncommon Pets*. New York: Holt, Rinehart & Winston, 1979.

ADULTS   Carrington, Richard, and the editors of Time. *The Mammals*. New York: Time-Inc., 1963.

Elementary Science Study. *Animals in the Classroom: A Book for Teachers*. New York: McGraw-Hill, 1970.

Murie, Olaus J. *A Field Guide to Animal Tracks*. Boston, Mass.: Houghton-Mifflin, 1975.

Animals: Reptiles, and Amphibians

CHILDREN   Billings, Charlene W. *Salamanders*. New York: Dodd, Mead, 1981.

Blassingame, Wyatt. *Wonders of Frogs and Toads*. New York: Dodd, Mead, 1975.

Graham, Ada, and Frank Graham. *Alligators*. New York: Delacorte Press, 1979.

Fitcher, George S. *Keeping Amphibians and Reptiles as Pets*. New York: Franklin Watts, 1979.

Patent, Dorothy H. *Reptiles and How they Reproduce*. New York: Holiday House, 1977.

Zim, Herbert S. *Alligators and Crocodiles*. New York: William Morrow, 1978.

———. and Robert M. Smith. *Reptiles and Amphibians*. Golden Guide Series. New York: Western, 1953.

ADULTS   Cochran, Doris, and Coleman J. Cochran. *The New Field Book of Reptiles and Amphibians*. New York: G.P. Putnam's Sons, 1978.

Conant, Robert. *Field Guide to Reptiles and Amphibians of Eastern and Central North America*. Boston, Mass.: Houghton-Mifflin, 1975.

Water

CHILDREN   Arnov, Boris. *Water: Experiments to Understand It*. New York: Lothrop, Lee & Shepard Books, 1980.

Couffer, Jack, and Mike Couffer. *Salt Marsh Summer*. New York: G.P. Putnam's Sons, 1978.

Engel, Leonard. *The Sea*. Young Readers Library. New York: Silver Burdett, 1977.

Leopold, Luna B. *Water: A Primer*. Geology Series. San Francisco, Calif.: W.H. Freeman, 1974.

Pringle, Lawrence. *The Minnow Family*. New York: William Morrow, 1976.

Reid, George K. *Pond Life*. Golden Guide Series. New York: Western, 1967.

ADULTS   Klots, Elsie B. *The New Field Book of Freshwater Life*. New York: G.P. Putnam's Sons, 1966.

Physical Environment

CHILDREN   Adams, George F., and Jerome Wyckoff. *Landforms*. Golden Guide Series. New York: Golden Press, 1971.

Bendick, Jeanne. *Putting the Sun to Work*. New York: Garrard, 1979.

Coburn, Doris. *A Spit is a Piece of Land: The USA Landforms*. New York: Julian Messner, 1978.

Farb, Peter, and John Hay. *Face of North America. The Natural History of a Continent*. New York: Harper & Row, 1963.

Gallant, Roy. *Earth's Changing Climate*. New York: Four Winds Press, 1979.

Kiefer, Irene. *Energy for America*. New York: Atheneum, 1979.

Pringle, Lawrence. *Nuclear Power: From Physics to Politics*. New York: Macmillan, 1979.

Rand McNally. *Our Magnificent Earth*. New York: Rand McNally, 1979.

Rhodes, Frank H. T. *Geology*. Golden Guide Series. New York: Golden Press, 1971.

Watson, Jane Werner. *Alternative Energy Sources*. New York: Franklin Watts, 1979.

Weiss, Malcolm E. *What's Happening to Our Climate*. New York: Julian Messner, 1978.

ADULTS   Congdon, R. J., ed. *Introduction to Appropriate Technology*. Emmaus, Pa.: Rodale Press, 1977.

Major, Ted. *Snow Ecology Guide*. Colorado: Thorne Ecological Institute, 1980.

National Geographic Book Service. *Our Continent*. Washington, D.C.: National Geographic Society, 1976.

Stokes, Donald W. *A Guide to Nature in Winter: Northeast and North Central North America:* Boston, Mass.: Little, Brown, 1976.

Terry, Mark, and Paul Witt. *Energy and Order, a High School Teaching Sequence*. San Francisco, Calif.: Friends of the Earth Foundation, 1976.

Watts, May Theilgaard. *Reading the Landscape of America*. New York: Macmillan, 1975.

ACTIVITY GUIDES   *Energy 80*. Los Angeles: Enterprise for Education, 1981. Booklets for students and *A Teacher's Guide to the Energy 80 Student Booklet,* available upon request. This program is funded by businesses in several states, and in-service training is available in California, Massachusetts, Oklahoma, and plans are underway for Texas.

Tully, Randolph R., Jr., with D. Chris Reese. *Counting on Energy*. Blue Bell, Pa.: Project E3, 1980. Activities suitable for a range of grades and skills, including data sheets, worksheets, teaching notes, and activity suggestions on the following topics: human energy, electricity, space heating, solar energy, and bioconversion.

7 · Enrichment Ideas Workshop

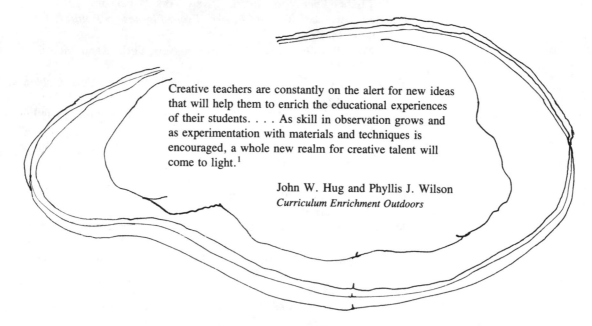

Creative teachers are constantly on the alert for new ideas that will help them to enrich the educational experiences of their students. . . . As skill in observation grows and as experimentation with materials and techniques is encouraged, a whole new realm for creative talent will come to light.[1]

John W. Hug and Phyllis J. Wilson
Curriculum Enrichment Outdoors

There will be times when you have planned an environmental experience outdoors but cannot go there because the area is already occupied or the weather is much too inclement. Or you may be in a very limiting setting and can provide more experience for your students by collecting natural materials for use in the classroom. With very little notice and some imagination, an outdoor theme can be carried on indoors using nature crafts, games, and activities. It is hoped that some hands-on field experience can be added at another time.

ENVIRONMENTAL GAMES

Games are an important learning device and an integral part of our culture. Ideally, games with an environmental theme should be used in conjunction with other types of learning to reinforce ongoing studies.

The games presented in this workshop are simple and can be used both indoors and outdoors. They are multidisciplinary and allow the integration of environmental themes into a variety of subject areas. Many of the games emphasize the senses and deemphasize competition. It is a good idea for the leader to try out the game on family and friends before adapting it to the needs of a particular group.

ENVIRONMENTAL CRAFTS

Crafts, using natural materials, can encourage a knowledge of the environment by emphasizing the abundance and/or scarcity of particular items in your area. In addition, taking advantage of nature's seasonal discards (e.g., seeds, leaves, cones, driftwood) can lead to an understanding of seasonal change. Many students who do not concentrate well indoors or outdoors when doing serious investigations enjoy applying their practical skills to producing art objects. Working with natural materials leads to conversations about where the material was collected. Students may be guided in learning to collect judiciously. The object used can be referred to by name, for example, the "pine cone" or the "milkweed pod." This will enable students to communicate what they have learned to others because they will know the names of their materials. Craft projects can spark enthusiasm for outdoor investigation of the living plant.

Native American projects using natural materials collected outdoors can stimulate an appreciation for ways in which raw materials meet basic needs. Traditionally, native Americans were entirely dependent upon the materials of nature for their homes, tools, and household implements, which were made from wood, stone, shell, bone, and other natural materials. The life-style of native Americans reflect their deep appreciation for the complexity and interdependency of all living things.

Modern technology allows people today to combine Nature's materials to create new objects. For example, sand and water, both natural materials, are made into glass. However, this often causes a problem because man-made objects are slower to break down in the environment.

Craft projects should also involve the use of man-made litter to focus attention on the types of litter people create and how they dispose of it. Making an art object out of an old bottle, tin can lids, or metal pull-up tops, can stimulate discussion about Nature's way of breaking down materials (see Figure 7–1).

Figure 7–1
"Woman Bending"
(Coat hanger, button, thread, and film)

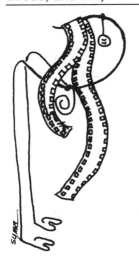

ENRICHMENT ACTIVITIES

WEB OF LIFE GAME

Purpose To develop simple food chains and webs.

Equipment Reference books; file cards.

Activity Each student draws or writes the name of one plant or one animal on a file card. Duplication does not matter. Students should know something about the animal—what it eats and what eats it. Then the students start arranging cards in simple food chains, as shown in Figure 7–2, using reference books to supplement their knowledge.

Figure 7–2 Simple Food Chain

At this point, if not before, it will become apparent that something else is needed to turn the simple food chain into a closed cycle. Cards for decomposers can be made now. Young students will each enjoy holding a card and arranging themselves in order. Above fourth grade, they will probably prefer to lay the cards out in the pattern. For this purpose a very large sheet of paper or a floor on which chalk marks can be made is helpful. See Figure 7–3 for a possible arrangement.

Figure 7–3 Complex Food Chain

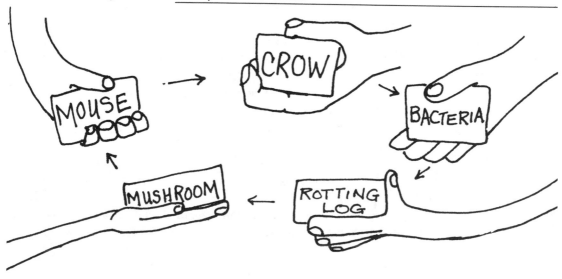

In addition to students discovering a few possible cycles from their organisms, they have probably observed more complex patterns. The fact will emerge that the interrelationships actually constitute an interlocking and overlapping web.

Teacher Tips   At about grade three or four, children know what animals and plants inhabit particular areas (from reading, field observations, films, and slides), and they are ready to understand the interrelationships of plants and animals.

ARTS AND CRAFTS   **Purpose**   To encourage discretion in the use of natural materials and to promote cooperation and sharing.

Figure 7–4
Dried Materials
in Container

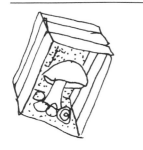

Equipment   Natural materials, lumber, sandpaper, clay, glue, crayons, pencils, cardboard, yarn, fabric, coat hangers, paint.

Activities   Have students do the following activities.

1. Attach pieces of bark, driftwood, seed pods, mushrooms, and so on, onto shingles or pieces of old wood for attractive wall hangings.
2. Build small boxes and line them with sandpaper as a backdrop for a variety of dried materials such as shells, mushrooms, grasses (see Figure 7–4).
3. Make vases or weed holders out of natural clay, and arrange them with dried flowers and grasses.
4. Make sachets filled with flower petals that have been dried.
5. Draw an animal or a plant and fill in the figure by gluing in natural material, such as beans or broken shells. This activity is particularly good for preschool and kindergarten children.
6. Make a variety of rock animals by collecting and assembling different shaped rocks, or make a rock mosaic. Use fast-setting glue. (See Figure 7–5).
7. Make leaf rubbings by laying a thin sheet of paper over a fresh leaf and gently rubbing with a crayon or lead pencil until the veins of the leaf or stalk appear. (See Figure 7–6.)

Figure 7–5
Rock Turtle

Figure 7–6   Pine Needle Rubbing

Figure 7–7   Cardboard Loom

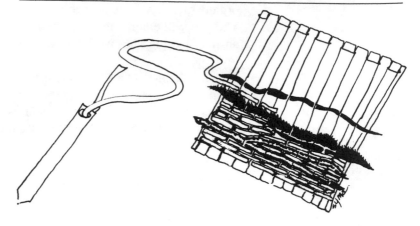

8. Make a simple cardboard loom strung with yarn. Weave pieces of grass, strips of bark, and so forth, under and over the yarn to make a wall hanging. (See Figure 7–7.)
9. Take strips of burlap, velvet, flannel, or colored ribbons and arrange dried flowers along the material.
10. Make a set of balance beams using a wire coat hanger and a couple of boxes or pails for math class.
11. Collect shells and arrange them in the shape of flowers or other objects.
12. Decorate pumpkins and gourds by drawing on them and/or cutting them out.
13. Make rattles and cups out of gourds. Cut them and dry them slowly in the sun.
14. Use shells to construct a variety of little animals, boats, or funny people.
15. Collect pine cones from a variety of evergreen trees and make wreaths, candle holders, cone flowers, pine cone people, and birds. Or fill the pine cones with peanut butter and seeds and hang them out for the birds.
16. Locate local clay or purchase clay and press natural materials into the clay for permanent impressions. Also, make pendants, wind chimes, and trivets. (See Figure 7–8.)
17. Make spatter prints of leaves by pinning a leaf to a piece of paper and spattering paint around the rest of the paper. When the leaf is removed an image remains. Make notepaper or bookcovers with these prints.
18. Glue dried flowers and weeds to paper to make fancy note paper.
19. Collect materials from the community and create art works. Emphasize how important it is to collect judiciously so that plants are not damaged, animal homes are not destroyed, and

ENVIRONMENTAL EDUCATION

Figure 7–8   Clay Items

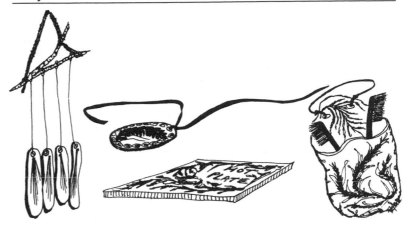

plant roots are left undisturbed. Have each piece of art show the following:

a. How beautiful is the environment
b. How ugly is the environment
c. How the environment makes you feel
d. How happy your environment makes you
e. How sad your environment makes you
f. How time has changed your environment

The quality of the local environment can be judged based on student impressions. As a group, discuss what factors make up a pleasing environment.

Teacher Tips

1. Before starting a craft project, make a list of the materials that might be used attractively.
2. Discuss where the material may be found, and include as much discussion about the natural environment as possible.
3. *Remember:* In the past craft books may have encouraged collecting too many, and often rare, materials. Use discretion when choosing craft books.

INDIAN LORE   **Purpose**   To acquire an appreciation for the way native Americans used the plants, animals, and minerals in their environment to meet their needs. To develop skills in identifying and manipulating these natural materials.

Preparation   Obtain permission to collect materials in the community, or ask students to collect materials at or near home to prevent overuse of any one area.

Equipment

Activity 1. Scissors, string, needle, and thread.

Activity 2. Pail, shovel, clay, hammer, one-eighth-inch wire screen, water.

Activity 3. Stones.

Activity 4. Chicken bones, pot of boiling water, Axion, pipe cleaners, drying rack, macrame cord, assorted beads.

Activity 5. Shells, hammer, file or sandpaper, pump drill, macrame cord.

Activities

Figure 7–9
Cattails

1. Native Americans sewed cattail leaves together for mats to cover their wigwams and to line the floors of their homes. They used the seeds from the brown flower spikes as home-insulating material and as diaper material in the baby's cradleboard. Many parts of the plant were harvested to eat, for example, the new shoots from the rootstock, the male blossom at the top of the flower stalk, and the root. See Figure 7–9.

    Take a walk with students in a marshy area where cattails flourish. Have students cut open a leaf to see the large holes that carry the water up through the plant during growing season. As the leaves dry, they shrink. Have each student cut one leaf to bring inside to dry in a cool place. When the leaves are dry, they can slit them with a fingernail into three sections. Soak the sections in warm water, and braid the pieces together. The leaf is very strong and will make a rough little braid that can be wound in a circle and sewed together like a braided rug.

2. Native Americans fashioned containers out of clay dug from the earth. With students look for clay deposits in the community and collect enough for them to make a small pot or bowl as follows. Remove as much debris as possible from the clay at the site. Allow the clay to dry out completely, then pound it into a fine powder. Put the powder through a one-eighth-inch screen to remove all tiny pebbles, twigs, and pieces of grass. Add just enough water so the clay holds its shape when formed into a ball. Knead the clay for as long as your hands have strength. Well-kneaded clay is the most satisfying to work. Mold the clay over a large rock or other object and allow it to dry; or model it by pinching a hole in the center of a clay ball and pressing and stretching it into shape. Allow the pot to dry in a cool place. (Quick drying will cause the clay to crack.) When the pot is completely dry, it can be fired in a kiln or set in a well-heated fireplace.

3. The Native American's tool box consisted of tools made out of a variety of materials: Stone, bone, shell, antler, and wood were among the most common. Throughout North America stones were collected and traded for their unique characteristics. It takes a great deal of skill to make sophisticated stone tools, but simple tools can be made from stones collected anywhere. Students can collect stones and experiment with how they might be used. Does the shape suggest a hammer? Cutting blade? Chisel? Could the stone be worked into another form? What kind of a tool? Tell students to strike two stones together and see if either one fractures. What does this tell them? Remind students to wear eye goggles when working stone as flakes can fly off and strike the eyes.

4. Animal bones provided the Native American with materials for tools and ornaments. Bone is easy to work and is durable. It was particularly suited for tools that required both strength and resiliency. When bleached and combined with other materials, bone makes an attractive ornament.

   As a class activity, boil chicken wings in 2 tablespoons of Axion for about 1 hour. Axion will make the bones white and shiny. Clean the marrow out of the center of the bones with a pipe cleaner, and allow bones to dry overnight. String the bones on a cord, interspersing them with wood, ceramic, or seed beads to make a necklace or bracelet.

5. Shells were used for tools and ornaments by native Americans. Many large marine shells make natural containers. Shell ornaments had long-standing importance among tribes as symbols of wealth and position.

   Students can collect shells from the seashore or lake or ask for discards at the local fish market. Salt water mussel shells are very attractive, and students can make lovely necklaces from them. Break a mussel shell into irregular pieces with a hammer, and file the edges smooth. Drill a hole in the shell and tie it to a cord to make a pendant. See Figure 7–10.

**Figure 7–10
Mussel Shell**

Follow-Up Read a Native American anthology, and compare attitudes of Native Americans toward the environment to attitudes of people from industrial societies.

SOUND AND MUSIC **Purpose** To encourage an appreciation of the natural world through the sense of sound.

Equipment Tape recorder, record player, records; rhythm sticks, bottles, wash tubs, cans, rubber bands, boxes, wood scraps, straws, or other recycled items.

Activities The following activities may be done with your students.

1. Sharpening perception
   a. Listen for rhythms in cricket and bird songs.
   b. Attempt to match the rhythms on rhythm sticks.
   c. Imitate animal and plant (leaves rustling) sounds vocally or with simple instruments.
   d. Record several minutes of outdoor sounds on tape at the same time the students are listening to these sounds. Have the students list as many of the sounds as possible, and then play the tape to see who heard the most.
   e. Have the students lie quietly on their backs in the grass for 5 minutes with eyes closed. Then, talk about what they heard.
   f. Have them lie on their stomachs and do the same thing. Are there differences in what they heard?
   g. Play hearing games. For example, turn your back to class and drop different items onto the desk. The students must guess the names of the objects.
   h. Discover how different animals make noises. Sneak up on crickets and grasshoppers. Build mini-animal environments to bring sounds into the classroom.
2. Musical and dramatic interpretation
   a. Make a list of current popular and familiar songs that deal with the environment.
   b. Sing nature songs and environmental protest songs. Obtain copies of written ones, and make up some of your own.
   c. Identify as many of nature's instruments as possible: wind-playing telephone wires, woodpecker drummers, and so on.
   d. Make up words to match bird songs. Do robins necessarily say, "Cheerily, cheerily?"
   e. Set Haiku to music.
   f. Play a record of sounds in nature (insects, frogs, birds) and ask students to raise their hands if they recognize sounds.
   g. Make instruments out of solid waste and natural materials. (See Figure 7–11.)
   h. Listen to classical music and have students write or draw what the music suggests.
   i. Make up a "sound effects" story.
   j. Make up musical stories without words, using simple instruments.
   k. Play records (e.g., Seeger and Lehrer) dealing with the environment.
   l. Write a conservation play with music.

Figure 7–11   Musical Instruments

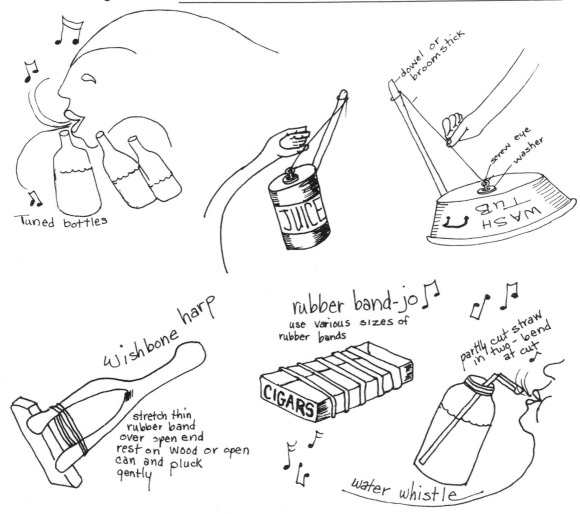

Tuned bottles

dowel or broomstick
screw eye
washer
WASH TUB
JUICE

wishbone harp
stretch thin rubber band over open end rest on wood or open can and pluck gently

rubber band-jo
use various sizes of rubber bands
CIGARS

partly cut straw in two - bend at cut
water whistle

m. Choose music for silent films and film loops and coordinate them.
n. Show movies that have no narrative and discuss.
o. Discuss the kinds of sounds that suggest different moods, and have students try to make these sounds.
p. Identify familiar games that have an environmental basis: Fox and Geese; Run Sheep Run; Monkey See, Monkey Do.

ECOLOGY   **Purpose**   To involve students in direct experiences outdoors.

Equipment
Activity 2.   World map, colored pins, string.
Activity 3.   Twigs, leaves, flowers, seeds, scissors, glue, cardboard.

Activity 4.   Seeds.
Activity 5.   Seeds, blotter, pieces of glass, hand lens.
Activity 6.   Glass jar, paper towels, seeds.
Activity 7.   Leaves, twigs, stones, galls, bag.
Activity 10. Terrarium, oatmeal, coffeegrounds, milk.
Activity 11. Screen, plastic lids, plaster.
Activity 12. Screen, jar lid, flower pot.
Activity 13. Aquarium.
Activity 14. Bulletin board.
Activity 15. Freshly cut log.
Activity 17. Flannel board.
Activity 18. Recycled materials.

Activities

1. *Have students invent a name for a plant or animal* based on appearance and/or where it lives and what it needs. For example, if the plant has a tall pointed stalk, has many tiny purple flowers, grows in wet areas, and grows in masses, *I call it* "Purple Steeple." (The name of this plant is Loosestrife.) Armed with observed information, students will be able to look up the real name after they have invented their own to see if they are close. Looking up the item will enable students to learn more about it.

2. *Put a large world map on the board.* Give each student a set of colored pins or colored thumb tacks. Assign each student a different bird and have him or her insert one pin in the bird's most northern spot and a second pin in the bird's most southern spot. The student can loop up the principal route of the bird and, using a piece of thread, tie the string along that route connected by his or her pin colors. The next student can do the same thing. Numerous routes will cross, and it will be evident that migration routes can get quite complex after many birds have been traced. Information about bird migration may be found on "Bird Migration, Chart L" (from the National Audubon Society, 1130 Fifth Avenue, New York, New York 10028). This is a very good geography exercise and is suitable for students from grade four up.

3. *Collect a variety of twigs, leaves, flowers, seeds,* and so forth, and cut them in half. Glue one-half of each to a cardboard, and hand out the remaining halves. Have each student match his or her half of the item to one on the cardboard. Include two very similar items such as two varieties of maple leaves. Students will have to make keen observations before making a decision.

4. *Collect a variety of different seeds,* and hand them out to the students. Ask them to guess how the seeds might travel based on their appearances. (Acorns have to be carried;

dandelions and milkweed blow in the wind; burdock hooks onto clothing or fur; jewelweed shoots its seeds; and some seeds drop straight down to the ground.)

5. *Sprout seeds* by placing them on a moistened blotter. Place a piece of glass or plastic on top of the seeds on the blotter. Watch the seeds as they sprout. Use a magnifying glass to identify the tiny plant parts.

6. *Collect a glass jar, paper towels, and several large seeds.* The seeds can be made to sprout by filling the jar with rolled up, wet paper towels and placing a seed halfway down the jar using the crumbled wet towel to hold the seed in place. Add about one-half-inch water to the bottom of the jar. This method of sprouting allows the seed to grow in its natural upright position. The stem will go upward and the roots will go downward. It also simplifies watering. Plant several seeds and make comparisons.

7. *Fill a small bag with natural materials:* leaves, twigs, stones, insects, galls, and so forth. Tell where the items were collected: field, forest, or swamp? Have each student take one item from the bag and present arguments to the class about how it would be possible to remove the item permanently from its environment. The class must then dispute the arguments. For example, a student has a stone that was found in a field. The stone may appear unnecessary, but it provides a dark, moist place under which animals live; it is home for lichen and it will eventually break down to become soil. After several students have presented their items, it becomes apparent that every item is necessary to every environment and nothing should be removed.

8. *Adaptation is important* to all animal life. Students can develop an appreciation for how they differ from lower animals in an ability to grasp objects by taping their thumbs to their palms for several hours. Pass things around the room and have students try to eat. See how difficult simple tasks become. Make a list of things thumbs enable people to do that lower animals are deprived of doing.

9. *A concept of community* is important to all animal life. Create a mock trial to explore community interdependence. For example:

CAST OF CHARACTERS	Jenifer Grey Birch, Flora Fungus, Walter Wintergreen, Wayne Woodpecker.
CHARGES	Flora Fungus is accused of murdering Jenifer Grey Birch by toppling her to the ground.
FACTS	Jenifer Grey Birch is from a long line of

healthy birches who have lived for many years in this woodland habitat.

As a rotting log, Jenifer Grey Birch will enrich Walter Wintergreen's habitat and will create additional food sources for Wayne Woodpecker.

Flora Fungus argues that Jenifer Grey Birch was already old and sickly when she came to live with her.

QUESTION Is Flora Fungus guilty of murder?

Have a jury of students weigh and examine the evidence to decide the case. (Use any cast of characters familiar to the students.)

10. *Dig for earthworms* and build a terrarium using materials from the earthworm's natural habitat. Earthworms live in moist grassy places and are often found under a pile of decaying leaves and insects, which they help to grind up. Look for castings that are a combination of soil and organic material that the worm has ingested, ground up, and excreted as pellets. Near the castings are the burrows where the worms can be found. Earthworms can be kept alive in a terrarium by adding organic material from their natural habitat or by feeding them from the following mixture: one-half cup raw oatmeal, one-half cup coffee grounds, and 1 tablespoon milk.

11. *Build a cricket cage* and catch a cricket. Crickets like to eat other insects and plants including table vegetables, apples, and wet bread. Have students watch the movement of the cricket and imitate its song and dance.

12. *Build a grasshopper cage* as shown in Figure 7–12 and catch a grasshopper. Grasshoppers like apples, celery, and lettuce. They need water. Do not put a grasshopper into a cricket cage. The cricket might eat the grasshopper.

Figure 7–12   Grasshopper Cages

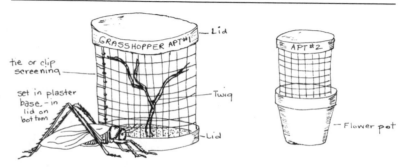

13. *Build an aquarium* and collect plants and animals from a local pond or stream. Directions for building an aquarium can be found in Chapter 6.

14. *Keep a bulletin board* of natural history events. Have the class post seasonal happenings. For example, spring—red-winged blackbird sighted near First Street or tulips out around town hall. Encourage students to write up their own observations for posting. If students are aware that a seasonal event is likely to occur have them post a WANTED sign on the board. Others can be on the lookout for the wanted item.

15. *Bring in a freshly cut log* for students to study. Have them count the rings and try to determine the age of the tree. Were some years better growing years than others? (This can be seen by the width of the ring, i.e., thin lines indicate poor growing years, thick lines good ones.) Determine in what year the tree was planted.

16. *Have students choose a plant or animal* with which they are familiar. Have them write a poem describing the development of that plant or animal based on what they know about it. For example, "I used to be a winged seed, but now I am a maple tree." Or, "I used to be a brown and black caterpillar, but now I'm just a small light moth."

17. *Make a flannel board* for younger students to illustrate a nature story. Cover a board with felt and make felt animal and plant cutouts to attach to the board. Encourage students to write their own stories and to create their own characters in felt. Assemble a picture on the board and have the students write a nature story to go with it.

18. *Invent an animal* that can adapt to particular environments, seasons, or conditions. Discuss seasonal changes and how animals adapt to them. Have students make a model from an assortment of recycled materials, and let them explain how the invented animal adapts. Figure 7–13 shows an invented animal adapted to winter.

Figure 7–13   Invented Animal

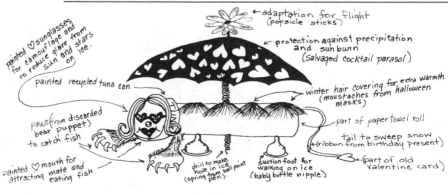

REFERENCES

Enrichment Ideas

CHILDREN   Benson, Kenneth R., and Carl E. Frankson. *Creative Naturecrafts.* Englewood Cliffs, N.J.: Prentice-Hall, 1968.

Cutler, K. N. *From Petals to Pinecones: A Nature Art & Craft Book.* New York: Lothrop, Lee & Shepard Books, 1969.

Gjersik, Maryanne. *Green Fun.* Riverside, Conn.: Chatham Press, 1975.

Hershoff, Evelyn G. *It's Fun to Make Things from Scrap Materials.* New York: Dover, 1964.

Hess, Lilo. *The Amazing Earthworm.* New York: Charles Scribner's Sons, 1979.

Hillcourt, William. *The New Field Book of Nature Activities & Hobbies.* New York: G.P. Putnam's Sons, 1978.

Richardson, Hazel. *Games for the Elementary School Grades.* Minneapolis, Minn.: Burgess, 1951.

————. 1957. *Games for the Junior & Senior High School.*

ADULTS   Chinery, Michael. *Enjoying Nature with Your Family.* New York: Crown, 1977.

New Games Foundation. *The New Games Book.* Garden City, N.Y.: Doubleday, 1976.

Peck, Ruth L. *Art Lessons that Teach Children About Their Natural Environment.* West Nyack, N.Y.: Parker, 1973.

ACTIVITY GUIDES   Gaudette, Marie E. *Leader's Nature Guide.* New York: Girl Scouts of the U.S.A., 1973.

Enrichment Ideas: Indian Lore

CHILDREN   Amon, Aline. *The Earth is Sore. Native Americans on Nature.* New York: Atheneum, 1981.

Wilken, Marne. *The Long Ago Lake. A Childs Book of Nature Lore and Crafts.* New York: Sierra Club Books/Charles Scribner's Sons, 1978.

Wolfson, Evelyn. *American Indian Utensils. Make Your Own Basketry, Pottery and Woodenware with Natural Materials.* New York: David McKay, 1979.

————. 1981. *American Indian Tools and Ornaments. How to Make Jewelry and Implements Out of Bone and Shell.*

ADULTS   Bennett, Dean B. *Maine Dirigo 'I Lead'.* Maine Studies Curriculum Project. Camden, Me.: Down East Books, 1980.

Massachusetts Educational Television. "People of the First Light." Seven half-hour programs about native Americans in southern New England with related materials designed for viewers from age nine to adult. Cambridge, Mass.

Whiteford, Andrew Hunter. *North American Indian Arts*. New York: Golden Press, 1973.

8 · Environmental Issues

> We travel together, passengers on a little space ship,
> dependent on its vulnerable supplies of air and soil; all
> committed for our safety to its security and peace,
> preserved from annihilation only by the care, the work,
> and I will say the love we give our fragile craft.[1]
>
> Paul Steiner, editor
> *Collected Wit and Wisdom of Adlai E. Stevenson*

COMMUNITY ENVIRONMENTAL ISSUES

Identify Issues

If you do not already know what environmental programs and
problems exist in your community, there are many possible
sources of identification. Here are just a few.

Get ideas on environmental problems from government officials, active citizens, conservation group leaders. Use the local
library. Read local newspapers on current programs and problems.
Check papers and bulletin boards for announcements of meetings
and hearings of local boards on environmental topics. Start attending them. Tune in to local television and radio public affairs
programs.

Get the Facts

Once the problems are identified and defined, the job of collecting
background information and organizing it begins. Figure 8–1 is a
model for a community environmental profile.

---

[1]New York: Pyramid Books, 1965, p. 125.

Begin by looking for general background information on environmental problems (see "Environmental Concerns" in references). Be sure to check school and public libraries. Get on a mailing list of at least one ecology action organization that issues newsletters, summaries of legislation, or other pertinent information on solving community environmental problems. (See Appendix A.) Contact state and federal agencies connected with environmental programs and standards.

Select an Environmental Problem

Analyze the background material and select one problem that concerns you the most. To see what is happening on this problem locally, find out what is being done currently, if anything, and by whom, in your community. Acquire local background information through newspapers, community reports, interviews, and field surveys. Research all the possible alternatives for solving the problem.

Work Up a Plan of Action

With background information on one local problem and research on possible alternative solutions, communicate your findings to others and/or become an advocate for a particular plan of action. Consider any or all of the following ideas.

Communicate the facts to others by speaking at meetings, writing articles or letters to the newspaper, and contacting officials.

Provide materials for display or for studies to libraries, schools, and other groups willing to encourage public education on the selected environmental issue.

Ask media sources (television, radio, newspapers) to provide more coverage of environmental conditions in general and your issue in particular. If they are already performing this kind of public service, let them know you appreciate it.

Look for individuals and groups already concerned with your issue.

Participate in the work of a committee concerned with the local problem, or organize a committee if none exists.

Work to get passage of a local bylaw or other action to deal with the problem; seek local enforcement of existing legislation if it already exists.

At election time, actively support qualified candidates. If

Figure 8–1   Community Environmental Profile

I.   Environmental issues—Describe status of Problem and Current Programs
   1.   Water supply _____
   2.   Water quality _____
   3.   Air pollution _____
   4.   Noise pollution _____
   5.   Sewage disposal _____
   6.   Solid waste disposal _____
   7.   Hazardous waste disposal _____
   8.   Preserving open space and natural features _____
   9.   Protecting endangered species and wildlife _____
   10.   Energy conservation _____
   11.   Recycling _____
   12.   Pesticide control _____
   13.   Others _____

II.   Community public agencies concerned with environmental problems and programs—Describe responsibility and present actions
   1.   Executive branch
         Board of selectmen,
         mayor, council_____
   2.   Conservation agency(s)_____
   3.   Park, recreation agency_____
   4.   Public works, engineering_____
   5.   Board of health_____
   6.   Planning board and zoning board of appeals_____
   7.   Other_____

Communication between these agencies? Coordination regarding environmental issues? Communication with state, federal agencies regarding environmental issues? Long-range planning and master plan for community? How is environmental quality included?

III.   Community private agencies concerned with environmental programs and problems—List area of concern and extent of activity
   1.   Land trust(s)_____
   2.   Garden club(s)_____
   3.   Sports group(s)_____
   4.   Conservation action group(s)_____
   5.   Citizen action group (League of Women Voters, PTA)
         _____
   6.   Service organizations_____
   7.   Business associations_____
   8.   Other_____

Do these groups cooperate with each other? With public agencies? If so, how?

IV.   Communication with public
   1.   Describe local press coverage on environmental issues—extent and quality.

2. List any bulletins or periodicals issued locally that include environmental issues and briefly describe content and quality.
3. Is there library coverage of environmental issues—book displays, programs?
4. Is there television and radio coverage of local issues?
5. Are there public forums?
6. What community adult education programs (e.g., newcomers, senior citizens) are available?

V. School programs related to community environmental issues
1. Levels involved: Elementary_____Junior High_____ Adult Education_____High School_____
2. Comment briefly on extent of school involvement with community (school site use, community field trips, community problem solving, use of people as resources, and so forth).
3. What are the ways in which schools communicate with community and vice versa?
4. What are the ways in which environmental education is being integrated into school system? See Chapter 4 for checklist.

---

local leadership is not sensitive to environmental problems, consider running yourself.

Work with existing community leadership as much as possible. Encourage cooperative efforts toward solving the problem.

Communicate to Others

Whether you are merely trying to provide information to others or you are advocating a solution based on your consideration of alternatives, communications skills will be important. Many plans of action have bogged down or backfired because the groundwork was not properly prepared.

It is important to learn how to ask questions and how to be a good listener. Look for feedback, pro and con, and try to understand objections to your point of view before attempting to refute them. There are usually degrees of difference in thinking. Do not polarize views on the issue. Seek common grounds wherever possible. Realize that you may have to make compromises yourself. Be sensitive to different values and respect differences. Give credit to others when it is due.

Organize Others

If you are interested in getting beyond advocacy of one particular issue to a larger community endeavor, you can work with other individuals and organizations to develop community ties and a sense of common purpose. Focus on projects of mutual interest. An interpersonal network is more effective than an impersonal, information-giving approach.

Help others to get organized and involved, and to communicate by keeping co-workers or supporters informed on progress. Involve others in helping to eliminate roadblocks and to overcome and answer objections. If possible, develop strategies for solutions that satisfy at least some of the critics' concerns. You may have to face the reality that you will have to do most of the work yourself.

With reliable information, a plan of action, good communication skills, and a cooperative network, the only missing ingredients for a successful program are enthusiasm, patience, and *courage!*

DEVELOPING PROBLEM-SOLVING SKILLS

Problem solving is an approach to understanding community environmental issues that allows all points of view and alternatives to be explored, that involves real-life situations rather than theoretical ones, and that attempts to find solutions and a plan of action.

Problem solving is a particularly useful approach for the junior high grades and up because the higher level skills of analysis, evaluation, and synthesis are honed in considering solutions and implementing plans of action. It prepares students to become responsible citizens who can make decisions for a healthy environment.

Younger students need more direction in approaching community problems, and the emphasis should be on developing awareness and sensitivity to the environment and on observation and collection of information useful in identifying problems. These skills build the groundwork that enables students later to have the concern as well as the ability to recognize and solve problems. Younger elementary students see problems in terms of their basic needs and understand experiences that are concrete and personal. As they begin to sharpen their observation and critical thinking skills, they are able to answer a question such as, "What would you like to see happen to the corner lot"? (E.g., make it a baseball diamond, woods to play in, playground equipment.)

Three different but related problem-solving models are summarized below.

Unified Science and Mathematics for Elementary Schools

Unified Science and Mathematics for Elementary Schools (USMES) is an interdisciplinary program, developed by the Educational Development Center, that involves elementary school children in tackling problems related to their school and community environment. Thirty-two units can be used in grades 1 to 8. The level at which the children approach the problems varies according to age and abilities. Examples of some problems are getting to school, lunchroom lines, playground management, classroom design, traffic patterns, and consumer goods.

The problems are "real" in that the following apply:

1. They have immediate, practical effects on students' lives.
2. They have no "right" answers.
3. They require students to use their own ideas about what the problem is and how to solve it.
4. They can be resolved by students.
5. They are "big" enough to require many phases of class activity for any effective solution.

The USMES' problem-solving units include skills in defining the problem, measuring, collecting data, analysis of data, discussion, trial of alternate solutions, clarification of values, decision making, group cooperation, and communication.

Environmental Encounters

Environmental encounters is a critical thinking approach, developed by William Stapp of the University of Michigan, that has been designed for all disciplines and grade levels of a school system. The emphasis in the early grade levels is on basic awareness and appreciation of the environment; it leads up to encounters in which older students explore and critically evaluate existing environmental problems in the community.

Stapp lists the steps in sequence for this problem-solving approach:

1. Define the problem or issue.
2. Become informed.
3. Identify alternate solutions.
4. Evaluate alternate solutions.
5. Develop a plan of action.

6. Implement the plan of action.
7. Evaluate the implementation.[2]

Environmental encounter activities, which cover ecological concepts and problem-solving skills are provided in the Environmental Activities Manual. Each activity lists objectives, and procedures.

A flood plain zoning encounter for a high school American Government class is given as an example.[3] Objectives include: (1) mapping the flood plains; (2) a written record of floods and flood damage over the past 60 years; (3) collection of local and state laws regulating flood plain zoning; and (4) identification of the power structure, that is, who regulates flood plain development and zoning policies? Stapp lists numerous ways to locate this information, including tours, interviews, and research into records. After information is collected, solutions for the development or preservation of flood plains are to be offered, considering all influences and interests. If solutions do not coincide with existing views of policy makers, a plan of action and implementation is drawn up. This could be publicizing information or presenting it to a hearing.

Whether or not the students remember specific information from these encounters is not important. The attitudes and problem-solving skills they develop will enable them to cope with other environmental issues they encounter in the future.

Environmental Problem Solving

The Institute of Environmental Education reports on another model, Environmental Problem Solving (EPS). Students in junior and senior high, especially, begin EPS by identifying problems in the school and community or by participating in awareness and skill development activities that familiarize them with their community and a problem-solving approach.

The amount of student responsibility and teacher supervision depends on the experience and level of the group involved. Students develop their own study questions or you can give them a general category. Students work alone or in a group (two to six members). Each project is discussed in class and approved before a 3-week long study begins. At the end of the study, each group reports its findings to the class. Throughout the project, written or oral progress reports are given.

[2]William B. Stapp and Dorothy A. Cox, eds., *Environmental Education Activities Manual*. (Farmington Hills, Mich., 1979), p. 17. Reprinted by permission.
[3]*Ibid.*, p. 631.

After students have had experience with learning problem-solving skills by using readily available resources such as the library, they are ready for their first community EPS. The teaching program may culminate in undertaking a classwide project on a local issue that works toward action or change in the community environment. Abilities to interview, research, write, do field work, and interact with the community are skills developed in these projects.

Examples of projects to be undertaken include determining the amount of solid waste a hamburger store generates in 1 hour, investigating what factors must be considered in selecting a home site, designing a drainage plan for a poorly drained athletic field, and assessing the maple sugar industry in one town and how weather influences production.

TEACHER ROLE   You are a resource person who assists students in exploring a particular community problem in organizing research, locating resource materials, and working on solutions. As a coordinator, you provide the problem–challenge and, when needed, open-ended questions and opportunities for student interaction and cooperation. You are concerned with developing student skills on how to solve problems, not on influencing the thinking about a particular solution.

VALUES CLARIFICATION

Today's students will become the decision makers of the future. They can be helped to understand how their own values affect their behavior and attitude toward the environment through values clarification activities.

Learning to make sound decisions for a healthy environment means understanding the underlying causes of environmental problems as well as their effects on the home, community, and world. People's values, as reflected in their styles of life, are a contributing cause of environmental deterioration today, yet the connection between these values and environmental consequences is not often made in educational programs.

Students can begin to make choices, weigh alternatives, and evaluate cause and effect, so that gradually they become more aware of the relationship of values to environmental issues. With this increased awareness comes a recognition of the individual contribution to and impact on the environment, which prepares students to make environmentally related decisions as adults.

Values clarification does not need to be taught as a separate subject but can be included in any other teaching program. Through questionnaires, opinion polls, surveys, group discussions, and role playing in the classroom and in the field, students can be involved in making choices that allow them to show or say "I feel," "I would rather," "I like best or least" and to understand that others may have different opinions and values.

In the reference work, *Values Clarification: A Handbook of Practical Strategies for Teachers and Students,*[4] sample approaches and activities are given that allow students to express their opinions and choices in a variety of ways. A few examples include:

> Letters to the editor
>
> Interview of class members willing to give opinions in front of classmates.
>
> Choices (e.g.: Which do you identify with more, asphalt or grass?)
>
> A values continuum, or choice within a range of feeling (e.g.: Regarding the question, "How do you feel about hunting animals"? indicate position where you place yourself on a line ranging from "It is okay to wipe animals out" to "Let us make hunting illegal.")
>
> Attitude surveys that offer a chance to check statements according to: Strongly Agree, Agree, Undecided, Disagree, Strongly Disagree
>
> A values survey (e.g.: Which environmental problem are you most concerned about? Mark in order of importance: population control, air pollution, and so forth)
>
> The pie of life, in which each student divides up his or her day according to how time is spent (or similar division of priorities according to interests)
>
> An auction (e.g.: If you had so much money, how would you allocate it?)

These activities can encourage an expression of values without an emphasis on right or wrong. They can provide opportunities for students to share opinions and clarify their reasons for holding them.

Older students may be considering controversial environmental problems within their community in which there are conflicts of interest and value clashes. There may be strong differences of opinion within the class or within the community. If value clarification is part of their education, the students will want to understand the values of others as well as clarify their own. Avoid

---

[4]Sidney B. Simon, L. W. Howe, and H. Kirschenbaum, *Values Clarification: A Handbook of Practical Strategies for Teachers and Students.* (New York: Hart, 1972).

judgments of right and wrong while helping students develop skills in analyzing positions of all sides. Environmental problems are complex in nature, and differences of opinion must be expected and respected. Making connections between human beliefs and actions and their effects on the environment promotes responsible decision making.

VALUES CLARIFICATION ACTIVITIES

ENVIRONMENTAL ATTITUDES SURVEY

Purposes   To determine attitudes of students on statements about the environment. To encourage students to discuss reasons for opinions and to clarify feelings.

Equipment   Environmental Attitudes Survey (Figure 8–2)

Activity
1.   Pass out survey sheets which contain 25 statements about the environment. Have students circle the appropriate letter (A-Agree, U-Undecided, and D-Disagree) before each statement.
2.   Review answers to determine which statements cause the most difference of opinion, and which ones most students are undecided about.
3.   Find out if there is class interest in learning more about any of the most controversial or undecided statements.

Teacher Tips   Assist students in finding ways to clarify their opinions and to respect other's opinions.

ENVIRONMENTAL AUCTION

Purposes   To help students clarify priorities and use valuing processes. To stimulate dialogue about environmental issues.

Equipment   Environmental Auction (Figure 8–3) sheets.

Activity
1.   Pass out auction sheets to the class. Each of the 20 items is to be sold at auction to the highest bidder, according to the following rules:
  a.   You have *none* of the items listed at present.
  b.   You have a total of $5,000 to spend.
  c.   You can spend no more than $2,500 on any one item.
  d.   Bids must open at no less than $50 and no more than $500, and must proceed by increments of no less than $50 and no more than $100.

Figure 8–2   Environmental Attitudes Survey

Here are 25 statements concerning the world in which we live. In front of each statement please circle the appropriate letter that indicates your own feeling about that particular statement.

A—Agree   U—Undecided   D—Disagree

A U D   1. Because of our skills and technology, we no longer depend upon the environment for our basic needs.

A U D   2. Plants use energy from the sun to make food.

A U D   3. Some of the poisons sprayed on plants are passed on to animals through food chains and food webs.

A U D   4. Wars have often been caused by disagreements over the use and ownership of natural resources.

A U D   5. Sandy soil is not very good for leaching beds.

A U D   6. When fuels are burned, they often release gases that harm living things.

A U D   7. We should only be concerned with our present standard of living. Future generations will be able to take care of their own.

A U D   8. Since the average amount of rainfall in the United States is relatively high, we do not have to worry about future water supplies.

A U D   9. A person living in the city does not need to worry about conservation problems.

A U D   10. We may be in danger of extinction because of what we are doing to the environment.

A U D   11. Something is not a resource for us until we use it.

A U D   12. We should be allowed to use our own land, woods, and waters in any way we wish.

A U D   13. We may either increase or decrease soil erosion.

A U D   14. Soil indirectly supplies most of our food, shelter, and clothing.

A U D   15. Conservation of our forests is not necessary since we already have substitutes for wood.

A U D   16. When natural resources are used up in one area, we can always move on to other areas.

A U D   17. Human beings are animals.

A U D   18. There is little I can do about conservation. I am only one person.

A U D   19. We do not learn very much from our own classmates.

A U D   20. When we live in groups, we must give up some things to get other things.

A U D   21. The government can take care of natural resources without involving people.

		A U D	22.	We do not need laws to help take care of the environment. We can do it on our own.
		A U D	23.	A beautiful and quiet environment is necessary for some people to be happy.
		A U D	24.	We do not need to think of the future to plan today's actions.
		A U D	25.	Our awareness of our environment is limited by the nature and use of our senses.

Figure 8–3   Environmental Auction

Auction items	Initial $5,000 Budget	Highest Amount I bid	Top bid
A long life free of illness			
Travel and tickets to any cultural or athletic events, as often as you wish			
Television			
An unspoiled natural setting for your home			
Complete self-confidence with a positive outlook on life			
A complete library for your personal use			
A happy family relationship			
An automobile			
A large fruit and vegetable garden			
A very satisfying love relationship			
The ability to speak many languages			
A chance to eliminate sickness and poverty			
Electricity			
A chance to preserve endangered species			
An understanding of the meaning of life			
Unlimited funds for the enjoyment of music			
A world without prejudice			
Commercially canned and frozen foods			
A world without air and water pollution			
Love and admiration of friends			

e. You are creating your environment. None of the items you buy can be shared with the other people in your group.

2. Find out if there is consensus about some of the most important items or whether priorities are very different. Are conflicts, such as a desire for an automobile and a desire for a world without air pollution, felt between priority values?

3. Students may object to the rules and procedures that mix tangible and intangible items and that place maximums and minimums on the bidding. They may object to the limitation of one person buying a priority item, such as clean air. Modify items and procedures in ways that seem appropriate to your group. Experiment to see what works best.

Teacher Tips Useful discussions can emerge concerning how values are analyzed and the difficulty in assigning relative importance to them. Accent values clarification and tolerance of differences.

If this activity is used as an introduction to an environmental study, you may want to repeat it at the end of the study to see if value priorities have changed.

ROLE PLAYING, SIMULATION, AND GAMES

A role-playing approach can be used as a vehicle for understanding environmental issues and how decisions are made concerning them. Role playing can be done as a game, a mock meeting, hearing, forum, or other ways that encourage the consideration of a real-life environmental problem by allowing students to get the feel of those involved with the problem. Role playing teaches as much about attitudes and communication as it does about the process of decision making.

Set up your own role-playing situation to fit your needs. Select a real community environmental problem that involves conflicts of interest and several possible courses of action. Avoid issues on which the class (or community) is already polarized.

Some of the general conflicts to be considered include private rights versus public interest; long-range versus short-range benefits and losses (and relative costs); development versus preservation; growth and convenience versus quality of the environment; jobs versus environmental pollution. There will be many types of discoveries about these conflicts, such as questions of degrees of difference, semantics, tradeoffs, and compromises, all of which are related to how decisions are made in real life.

For younger students short role-playing activities can be designed, such as an ant's eye view of the world, frogs or raccoons looking for food in a habitat, or attitudes toward playground use, to encourage empathy and personal involvement in the environment. For older students specific problem-solving issues that might be role played include proposals for location of a new highway, financing a new solid waste or sewage system, the building of a marina in the wetlands, a mosquito spraying program, the salting of the highways during winter storms, a multiple family zoning proposal, or diverting highway funds for public transportation and bicycle paths.

After the problem is defined and a simulation or accurate representation or model of the real problem is designed, you are ready to identify roles of the key organizations and decision makers involved. The motives and purposes of the role players need to be examined and background reports prepared.

Prior to the classroom role-playing situation, background material for representing different points of view can be gathered by the students through inquiry and research. Meetings with officials, attending meetings, and acquiring data from community reports can be helpful in making the role playing more meaningful and the solutions offered more realistic.

From upper elementary and continuing through high school, role playing can take on increasing complexity. There are many varieties of a basic role-playing approach that can be used. Much depends upon the time allowed, format chosen, critical thinking level of the students, and amount of background material available. Roles can be switched at certain points to encourage the understanding of more than one point of view. A large group can break into smaller groups to discuss alternatives and solutions before coming back to the class for a final evaluation. Some role-playing sessions can last for several hours or class periods, and participants can get a chance to explore fully the complexities of decision making and of changing behavior and attitudes. The evaluation at the end is often a productive way to understand how much was accomplished and how close to the real situation the simulation came. Suggestions for modification can be tried out in the next role-playing situation.

If you are looking for activities and games already available as ecology simulations, there are any number of kits, boards, computer exercises, and media presentations available in libraries or stores. A variety of simulation games can be chosen that duplicates the conditions of real environmental problems for each age level, group size, and learning process. (See References at the end of this chapter.)

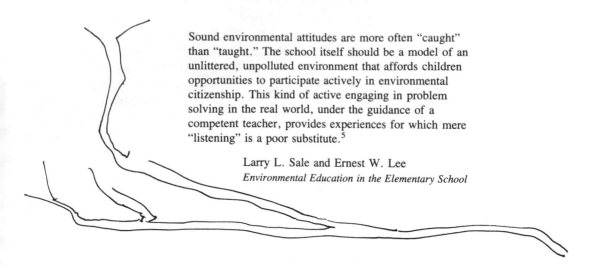

Sound environmental attitudes are more often "caught" than "taught." The school itself should be a model of an unlittered, unpolluted environment that affords children opportunities to participate actively in environmental citizenship. This kind of active engaging in problem solving in the real world, under the guidance of a competent teacher, provides experiences for which mere "listening" is a poor substitute.[5]

> Larry L. Sale and Ernest W. Lee
> *Environmental Education in the Elementary School*

ENVIRONMENTAL ISSUE ACTIVITIES

Below is a list of activities relating to environmental resources and problems, with an emphasis on the immediate environment (home, school, community), that the students can examine closely and of which they feel a part. Depending upon the age level and study objectives, these activities can be carried out through discovery, exploration, inquiry, problem solving, role playing, values clarification, or combinations of these learning approaches. Younger students can handle simple relationships between the self and the environment and can gradually learn to make connections. Older students are able to collect and analyze data, leading to discussions of alternatives and proposals for solution or improvement. The activities can tie in with the ecology concepts for each grade level outlined in Chapter 2.

1. In what ways do the students have their *basic needs* met? Discuss air, water, clothing, food, shelter, and transporta-

---

[5]© 1972 by Holt, Rinehart and Winston, Inc., page 41. Reprinted by Holt, Rinehart and Winston.

tion as human needs dependent upon natural resources from the environment.

2. Discuss how these *resources* are provided to meet students' needs. Which resources are renewable and which are non-renewable? (See Chapter 6.)

3. How many ways do the students depend upon the *sun* each day (directly or indirectly)?

4. Let students keep track of all activities during one day and then decide which ones are related to *essential needs*. Which natural resources were used most (renewable or nonrenewable)? Which created the most pollution? Trace materials used back to people and services that supplied them.

5. How do students know there is *air*? Can they see it, feel it, smell it? What affects the air? Consider how heat, light, wind, aerosol, trees all affect air quality. What is the air quality of your community? How much pollution is there and what are the sources?

6. Let the students keep track of *water uses* in one day. Develop a plan for rational use based upon what students feel is essential and what environmental conservation needs are felt.

7. Let a classroom faucet drip into a bucket for one day and measure the amount of *water* wasted. Think of consequences if every student wasted this much a day (use math problems to figure this out). Find out the per capita consumption of water in your school and community. Relate average rainfall to average water use.

8. From where does local *water* come? Is the supply dependable? Is it clean? If it is treated, what for? What constitutes a safe standard?

9. In what ways do all basic needs relate to *plants?* What is the significance of the saying, "Have you thanked a green plant today?" How can students thank plants?

10. Make a survey of school lunch *foods* for one day, and trace where they were grown or might have been grown. How were they processed and transported? What aspects of the environment were used to grow, process, and transport them?

11. Do the same with other *basic needs* and related school activities, for example, schoolroom materials and equipment, schoolroom heat and light, student clothing, student transportation. Make assignments for different groups.

12. The *requirements of the total school building* can be studied in terms of resource use and waste products. What natural systems are related to school maintenance functions (water, waste, light, power, and heat)? What relationship exists

between functions and structure of buildings and equipment? How does the school building relate to the school grounds environment?

13. Consider the *neighborhood* around the school site. Have students do a map or sketch of their neighborhood. Include personal aspects such as student's home, church, stores, and other important places for the student. Add natural features. Make a second map of the same area, imagining what it would have looked like before man-made features were added. Make a third map to indicate changes the students can remember in their lifetimes in the neighborhood (if you are new to the neighborhood, ask an older resident).

14. Ask students in what ways is the *school environment* similar to that of the community. Different? Is the school subject to the same rules and regulations as the community? Consider ways to change the school environment. What would the students change?

15. Look at the *land use* of your school site. Consider present conditions, management, balance between human use and land care. Talk to people who make decisions about the school site and help maintain the school site (principal, custodian, school committee representative).

16. Ask students to think of all the people who are trying to *protect the environment*. Start with their school. Have them thank them in person or in letters for their conservation attitudes and efforts to improve environmental conditions.

17. Look at the *school grounds* to see what is ugly and what is beautiful. Look at the community to see what beautification practices exist. Is there agreement in the class as to what is beautiful and what is ugly? Try the ugly/beautiful activity in Chapter 5.

18. Develop "action" projects to *improve the school environment* within and outside of the classroom. Litter pickup is often an onerous chore unless related to a classroom project, such as selecting a special spot on the grounds and being its caretakers or gardeners.

19. Have students choose a favorite place of *natural beauty,* and draw pictures of it from memory. Students can write a story about that place. Is it in their city or town? Could there be a place like it in their community? How would they protect it?

20. Students prepare a list of *conservation lands or open spaces* in their community. What group or groups are responsible for keeping the land open? Do people donate land to the community? Does the community vote to buy as much open land as possible? Would you say the community had a lot of open space or very little? Students can invite conservation

representatives into their classroom to discuss their community's open spaces and to identify the areas on a local map. Take a trip to a public conservation site.

21. Is there a *wildlife refuge* in the community? Are there wild animals students would like to see saved? Which would they put in a refuge? Why? What animals have people driven out of urban and suburban communities? How has this affected other animal populations?

22. Identify existing *wildlife* on the school grounds, and prepare a plan to improve habitat in an area suitable for maintenance and observation, in order to attract wildlife.

23. Identify school *noises*. Which sounds are natural? Which man-made? Which pleasant? Unpleasant? Which aid and which interfere with a good learning atmosphere? Where is the most noise control needed? Try experiments in and out of the classroom.

24. What forms of *pollution* do the students notice most? Have students keep a list over a period of 1 week of the ways the community and school are creating pollution. Encourage them to observe forms of pollution while walking or riding to and from school. Are there unattractive signs in town? Is the roadway littered with cans and bottles? Is there paper blowing all over the school grounds? Are some kinds of pollution harder to detect than others?

25. Investigate different kinds of *litter* in the neighborhood or on the school grounds. Collect it in a trashbag and try to identify what kind of material went into the litter. Classify litter as to its origin (natural or man-made) and kind. Make junk art such as mobiles or collages from the litter.

26. How much space can be saved if organic materials are put in a *compost heap?* Try a classroom compost experiment. What use could there be for the finished product?

27. Do a *survey of attitudes* in the community or have students ask own families. Do people feel strongly about the appearance of litter and the waste of resources? Do they recycle waste paper, bottles, cans, and so forth? If not, why not? Do they think recycling should be a voluntary program?

28. Interview teachers on *transportation* practices. Where do school faculty come from? What sources of transportation are available? What preferred? What used? How many riders are in each car? Make a census of car traffic in the school area.

29. Consider various means of *transportation* in terms of energy resources used. Jobs related to use? How is transportation related to energy, economic growth, and pollution?

30. Identify types of *energy* used in daily life. How does use

differ from country to city, from one section of the country to another, from season to season? Consider alternate sources of energy if one or more present sources is depleted. What energy using activities would students most readily give up?

31. Compare per capita *energy* use in United States with use per classroom student. Compare United States per capita use with that of a less-developed country. What are advantages and disadvantages of a style of life that uses increased energy consumption?

32. What is the present *population* of the community? Is it growing? What are estimates for the future? What are the causes of local changes in population? Discuss consequences. What is the space per person in the community today and what is the future estimate? What local zoning controls could determine population maximum? What other population controls such as on food and other resources, exist for people? How do other animals control population?

33. Consider *population problems* in a classroom exercise. For a brief time, several classes go into one classroom and share space and equipment. Or one class briefly goes into limited space inside or outside. What are their feelings about being crowded (air, heat, noise, peace of mind)? How could they feel if it were permanent?

34. List organisms *(pests)* harmful or distasteful to people (e.g., fleas, mosquitos) and discuss consequences of their effects on people. In what ways are they helpful to other organisms? Analyze various plans people use to control these organisms in school, community, and elsewhere and the effects on other organisms. Which organisms multiply as a result of human activity? House and fruit flies, cockroaches, and seagulls, for example, all like human garbage. Discuss control methods that are best for people and the environment. Is a balance possible?

35. Where does school *sewage* go? What system is used (septic, public treatment plant)? What are local, regional, and state laws concerning sewage? Are they enforced? What are the advantages of the present system? Problems? Alternatives?

36. Consider the *soils and drainage* on the school site in relation to the body of water into which it drains. Trace the water to the larger *watershed* system to which it belongs. Look at maps of the local watershed to understand how small streams drain into a larger water unit. Consider how the soil cover and slope of the land determine drainage patterns. After a storm take the students out on the school site and investigate the runoff. Look for small streams forming. What happens where there is hot top or pavement? Consider how trees and other plants help store water in the ground and prevent rapid

ENVIRONMENTAL EDUCATION

runoff and flooding. Look for examples of erosion, and consider ways to help control it.

37. On maps connect the local water supply and sewage system to the larger *watershed* system. Do the actions of other towns affect yours and vice versa? What happens when a stream is dammed? Filled in? How do ecological systems get out of balance due to water level or water quality changes? What food chains might be affected by removal of habitat?

38. Take a field trip to follow school ground drainage to local streams and to the larger *watershed*. See if there is a watershed agency that will send a field trip representative or provide written material.

REFERENCES

Environmental Concerns

CHILDREN   Koehler, Sherry, ed. *It's Your Environment*. New York: Charles Scribner's Sons, 1971–1976. (Anthology of *Eco-News* articles.)
Pringle, Laurence. *Only Earth We Have*. New York: Macmillan, 1969.
———. 1971. *Ecology: Science of Survival*.
———. 1975. *Energy: Power for People*.

ADULTS   *Annual Reports of the Council on Environmental Quality*. Washington, D.C.: Government Printing Office.
Carson, Rachel. *Silent Spring*. Boston: Houghton-Mifflin, 1962.
Commoner, Barry. *The Closing Circle*. New York: Alfred A. Knopf, 1971.*
Dubos, Rene. *So Human an Animal*. New York: Charles Scribner's Sons, 1968.*
Erlich, Paul R. *Human Ecology: Problems and Solutions*. San Francisco: W.H. Freeman, 1973.*
Man's Impact on the Global Environment: Assessment and Recommendations for Action. Cambridge, Mass.: MIT Press, 1970.
Schoenfeld, Clay, ed. *Interpreting Environmental Issues—Research and Development in Conservation Communication*. Madison, Wisc.: Dembar Educational Research Services, 1973.

Ecology Action

CHILDREN   Graham, Ada, and Frank Graham. *Careers in Conservation*. Sierra Club Scribner's Juvenile Series. New York: Charles Scribner's Sons, 1980.
Miles, Betty. *Save the Earth: An Ecological Handbook for Kids*. New York: Alfred A. Knopf, 1974.

*See other titles by same author.

ADULTS DeBell, Garrett. *The New Environmental Handbook*. New York: Friends of the Earth, 1980.

Environmental Action Coalition. *It's Your Environment. Things to Think About—Things to Do*. rev. ed. New York: Charles Scribner's Sons, 1976.

Griffith, Charles J., Edward Landin, and Karen Jostad. *EP—The New Conservation*. Arlington, Va.: Izaak Walton League of America, 1971.

Mitchell, John G., and Constance Stallings, eds. *Ecotactics: The Sierra Club Handbook for Environmental Activists*. Beaverton, Ore.: Touchstone Press, 1970.

Schoenfeld, Clay, and John Disinger, eds. *Environmental Education in Action. I: Case Studies of Selected Public School and Public Action Programs*. U.S. Education Resources Information Center, ERIC Document ED 141 185, 1977.

Tanner, R. Thomas. *Of Democracy and Courage: Studies of Environmental Action*. Case Studies and Spirit Masters. New York: National Audubon Society, 1977.

The Next Whole Earth Catalog. Access to Tools. New York: Random House, 1980, rev. 1981.

Problem Solving

ADULTS Hungerford, Harold R. *et al. Investigations and Action Skills for Environmental Problem Solving*. Champaign, Ill.: Stipes, 1978.

Institute for Environmental Education. *An Environmental Education Guide for Teachers*. Cleveland, Ohio, 1976.

Oregon Department of Education. *Handbook of Environmental Encounters*. U.S. Education Resources Information Center, ERIC Document ED 113 151, 1973.

Stapp, William B. "An EE Program (K–12), Based on Environmental Encounters." *Environment and Behavior* 3, no. 3 (1971): 263–283.

CURRICULUM GUIDES Biological Sciences Curriculum Study. *Research Problems in Biology*. New York: Oxford University Press, 1976. (Junior and Senior High)

Education Development Center. *Unified Science and Mathematics for Elementary Schools* (USMES). rev. ed. Newton, Mass., 1976.

Stapp, William B., and Dorothy A. Cox, eds. *Environmental Education Activities Manual*. Farmington Hills, Michigan, 1979. (Grades 1–8)

Values Clarification

ADULTS Harmin, Merrill, Howard Kirschenbaum, and Sidney B. Simon. *Clarifying Values Through Subject Matter: Applications for the Classroom*. Minneapolis, Minn.: Winston Press, 1973.

Resource Books for Values Education: An Annotated Bibliography. U.S.

Education Resources Information Center, ERIC Document ED 126 389, 1976.

Simon, Sidney B., L. W. Howe, and H. Kirschenbaum. *Values Clarification: A Handbook of Practical Strategies for Teachers and Students*. New York: Hart, 1972. (Good reference, but out-of-print.)

————. *Values, Concepts and Techniques*. Washington, D.C.: National Education Association, 1976.

————. and Jay Clark. *Beginning Values Clarification: A Guide for the Use of Values Clarification in the Classroom*. LaMesa, Calif.: Pennant Press, 1975.

Role Playing, Simulation and Games

ADULTS   Horn, Robert E., and Anne Cleaves. *Guide to Simulations—Games for Education and Training*. 4th ed. Beverly Hills, Calif: Sage, 1980. (Bibliography.)

Learning with Games: An Analysis of Social Studies Educational Games and Simulations. Boulder, Colo: ERIC/CHESS, 1973.

National Education Association, and William R. Heitzmann. *Educational Games and Simulations*. Washington, D.C., 1974.

Activities

CHILDREN   Wilson, Forrest. *City Planning; A Book of Games for Young Adults*. New York: Van Nostrand Reinhold, 1975.

ADULTS   Bennett, Dean B. *Yarmouth, Maine, Community Environmental Inventory*. U.S. Education Resources Information Center, ERIC Document ED 101 936, 1972.

Dickey, Miriam, and Charles E. Roth. *Beyond the Classroom*. Lincoln, Mass.: Massachusetts Audubon Society, 1971.

National Audubon Society. *A Place to Live*. Teacher and Student Manuals on Urban Ecology. New York, 1970.

Rash, Julie, and Patricia Markum, eds. *New Views of School and Community*. Washington, D.C.: Association for Childhood Education International, 1974.

Rich, Dorothy, and Beverly Mattox. *101 Activities for Building a More Effective School-Community Involvement*. Washington, D.C.: The Home and School Institute, 1976.

Roller, Lib. *Using the School and Community: An Environmental Study Area Handbook for Teachers in Elementary Schools*. U.S. Education Resources Information Center, ERIC Document ED 071 917, 1972.

Roth, Charles E., and Linda G. Lockwood. *Strategies and Activities for Using Local Communities as Environmental Education Sites*. Columbus, Ohio: ERIC/SMEAC, December 1979.

U.S. Department of the Interior. *All Around You: An Environmental*

Study Guide. Washington, D.C.: Government Printing Office, 1971.

Wurman, Richard S. ed. *Yellow Pages of Learning Resources*. Cambridge, Mass.: MIT Press, 1972.

CURRICULUM GUIDES   Environmental Science Center. *Give Earth a Chance Series*. Minneapolis, Minn., 1973. (Grades 5–9)

————. 1973. *Environmental Issues Series*. (Upper Elementary)

————. 1973. *Breaking Into Your Community*. (Junior and Senior High)

Examining Your Environment Series. *Pollution*. Toronto: Holt, Rinehart and Winston, 1971. (Grades 5–8)

————. 1972. *Mapping Small Places*. (Grades 5–8)

————. 1975. *Ecology in Your Community*. (Grades 5–8)

University of the State of New York. *Living Within Our Means: Energy and Scarcity. Environmental Education Instructional Activities*. (two vols) Albany, New York, n.d.

9 · Evaluation and Summary

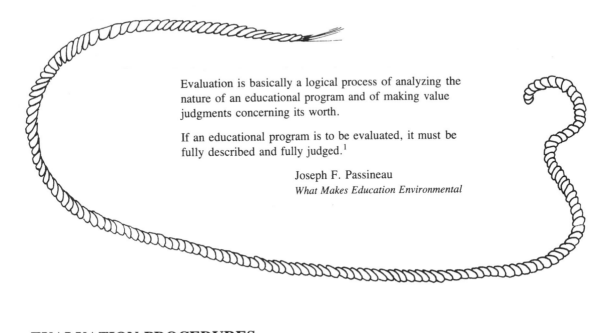

Evaluation is basically a logical process of analyzing the nature of an educational program and of making value judgments concerning its worth.

If an educational program is to be evaluated, it must be fully described and fully judged.[1]

Joseph F. Passineau
What Makes Education Environmental

EVALUATION PROCEDURES

The purpose of evaluating a program is to make it better. An environmental education training program must prove its worth in order to continue receiving support and funding. Three questions to consider in making this evaluation are:

1. Did the program fulfill its primary goals?
   a. To provide environmental education knowledge, skills, techniques, and practical teaching experience
   b. To encourage positive attitudes, self-confidence, and motivation to promote environmental education in the home, school, and community
2. Did the program serve participants' needs?
3. Are participants willing and prepared to use the training upon completion of the course?

As a participant you can answer these questions through filling out the evaluation forms, Figure 9-1, and through involvement in summary exercises.

---

[1]"Walking the Tightrope of Environmental Education Evaluation." (Washington, D.C.: Data Courier and Environmental Educators, 1975), pp. 371, 377.

Figure 9-1   Evaluation Questionnaire

Name of participant:_____   Date:_____

EVALUATION OF PROGRAM
1. What class sessions did you consider most helpful? Why? (Teaching or content?)
2. What class sessions did you consider least helpful? Why? (Teaching or content?)
3. Do you feel that additional information and training should be provided as part of this course? If so, what would you suggest?
4. What would you like to see offered as follow-up courses or supplementary workshops?
5. Please comment on the organization of the course (background material, order and emphasis of subjects, length of course, and so forth).
6. Please comment on homework assignments and time allotted for class discussion of them.
7. Please comment on opportunities for group interaction. Too many? Not enough?

REVIEW OF PARTICIPANT'S PROGRESS
1. Outline helpful teaching approaches outdoors.
2. Indicate why you feel teaching environmental education is important.
3. What guidelines for a good teacher aide and for aide/school relationships do you recommend?
4. Indicate recommendations for promoting environmental education in schools.
5. Indicate how you have used the information and contacts gained from this course to date. How could it be used in the future?
6. Indicate whether you would like a personal interview and assistance in getting started with a program in a particular school and/or in your community.

PERSONAL DIRECTION
What kind of role are you most interested in and are willing to play in promoting environmental education? Check your interests below, and double check any priority categories.

Working with Children

1. In schools as a paid teacher or teacher aide____ full time____ age level of children____ part time____
2. In schools as a volunteer____
   on a regular basis (e.g., two times weekly)____
   special programs (e.g., field trips)____
   after school programs____

3. With youth groups as a volunteer_____ or paid_____ after school activities_____ summer program_____
4. Other? List. _____

Not Working Directly with Children

1. In schools_____ In libraries_____ At home_____ Other_____
2. As a volunteer_____ As a paid worker_____ Full time_____ Part time_____
3. Type of work:
   Cataloging _____
   Preparing resource materials _____
   Research _____
   Audiovisual aids (slides, cassettes, and so forth) _____
   Curriculum planning _____
   Environmental education training and assistance _____
   Public information programs _____
   Political action on conservation problems _____
   Other? List. _____
4. If you have indicated that you want to be a volunteer, do you want to remain in this category or eventually become a paid worker?_____
5. If a paid worker, in what position? _____
6. Please list any particular skills, such as map making, photography, leading group singing, display preparation, dye making, special arts and crafts abilities.
7. Please list environmental education subject areas in which you feel most confidence, for example, plants, ecology, environmental quality issues.

While there are specific requirements for course attendance, homework preparation, and involvement in activities, there are no tests given to assess precise knowledge gained. However, the summary session does attempt, in a nonthreatening way, to insure that there are some basic understandings derived from the course.

COURSE SUMMARY QUESTIONS

The purpose of summarizing the course is to review the basic concepts and techniques presented and the skills developed. This can be demonstrated by your involvement in a series of exercises or discussion questions, with input by course leaders where necessary. Below are exercises and questions that could be used to review the environmental concepts and teaching techniques covered in this manual.

1. Describe an activity or game that encourages informality and group interaction to introduce environmental education to a new group.

2. What would you do with a group of 4-year-olds on their first sensory walk?

3. What basic ecology concepts are most important? Reach consensus through brainstorming technique.

4. You want to supplement your curriculum studies by taking your students out on the school grounds, but you do not know what is there. How would you begin to inventory your school grounds? How would you find out what information already exists about your school grounds?

5. You want to develop a nature trail. How would you plan stations so that students are involved in using discovery, exploration, and inquiry as part of their outdoor learning? How could you include the students in the planning and development of the nature trail?

6. You are a teacher or an environmental aide who has asked to be on the school committee agenda to discuss infusion of environmental experiences into the existing curricula. Give practical reasons for including environmental education and specific ways this could come about.

7. As a teacher, you would like to be able to use volunteers with environmental background; or as an environmental aide, you would like to assist a teacher in providing environmental experiences for students. What constitutes a cooperative teacher–volunteer relationship? What are rights and responsibilities of each?

8. You would like to take your class outside, but it is large and contains some very active and hard to manage students. What would you do to get extra help? How can you handle or avoid discipline problems outdoors?

9. Your class has been using first-hand learning experiences in the environment, while another teacher has been covering the same materials through a traditional lecture approach. How could you evaluate the two programs to compare strengths, differences in learning (in process and content)?

10. You have scheduled a field trip. What procedures and arrangements have you made to encourage a successful outing? What would you do when an unplanned event occurs, such as an accident or a "nature happening?" What and how would you plan for a rainy day activity to cover the same material?

11. Using the parking lot, devise a 10-minute environmental lesson for 10-year-olds.

12. Demonstrate simple approaches to classification and identi-

fication that stress outstanding characteristics, basic differences, and similarities.

13. Discuss several ways of presenting a pond life study, with merits and drawbacks of each. Cover research, teaching presentation, age level differences, materials, and equipment.

14. Pick a community or school problem and discuss steps by which students can develop a plan of action to solve it.

15. Suggest ways role playing can show how attitudes are important in reaching a decision on a community problem. What difficulties and challenges exist in dealing with values?

16. Your town needs to build a new school building. As a member of the planning committee, what architectural, environmental, educational considerations should affect the location of the building and the development of the site?

FOLLOW-UP

What kinds of questions and uncertainties still exist at the end of the course? What kinds of additional help and support do you need to use environmental education effectively?

The kind of follow-up needed will depend upon how ready you feel to begin using this training and what kinds of opportunities are available. Like most participants, you may benefit from additional workshops to reinforce learning after you have begun to apply your training and discover new needs. You may also benefit from keeping in touch with other participants and course leaders. Contribute to newsletters and participate in meetings that provide opportunities to share information on progress, problems, and experiences. This communication serves to increase motivation and confidence as well, and provides a supportive network.

REFERENCES

ADULTS   Bennett, Dean B. *Guidelines for Evaluating Student Outcomes in Environmental Education.* Yarmouth, Me.: Maine Environmental Education Project, 1973.

Fitz-Gibbon, Carol, and Lynn Lyons-Morris. *How to Design a Program Evaluation.* Beverly Hills, Calif.: Sage, 1978.

————. 1978. *How to Measure Program Implementation.*

McInnis, Noel, and Don Albrecht. *What Makes Education Environmental?* Louisville, Ky.: Data Courier and Environmental Educators. 1975.

Appendix A

Environmental Information Sources

Many private and public organizations produce excellent environmental materials at little cost. Regular newsletters, magazines, ecology-action bulletins, and services are often available from organizations by membership or request.

Below is a selected list of such organizations and a brief description of the materials and/or services they offer.

Private Agencies

Environment Action, Inc.
Suite 731
1346 Connecticut Avenue NW
Washington, D.C. 20036
    Action-oriented newsletter, including legislative and issue summaries

Environmental Action Coalition
235 East 49th Street
New York, New York 10017
    Urban-oriented materials, including *Eco-News* for students in grades 2 to 8

Friends of the Earth*
124 Spear Street
San Francisco, California 94105
    Monthly Newspaper, "Not Man Apart" on current environmental issues

League of Women Voters of the
U.S.*
1730 M Street NW
Washington, D.C. 20036
    Political action and education on issues, including natural resources, land use, and energy

National Audubon Society*
950 Third Avenue
New York, New York 10022
    Monthly magazine *Audubon* including news section; listing by state of *Directory of Nature Centers and Related Environmental Education Facilities*

---

*Check to see if organization has affiliate in your state.

National Wildlife Federation
1412 16th Street NW
Washington, D.C. 20036
  Monthly magazine *National Wildlife* and other information aids; *Ranger Rick* magazine for elementary students; annual *Conservation Directory,* including private and public organizations

Resources for the Future
1755 Massachusetts Avenue NW
Washington, D.C. 20036
  Free quarterly newsletter on environmental resource issues; research on environmental concerns

Scientists' Institute for Public Information (SIPI)
355 Lexington Avenue
New York, New York 10017
  Science-oriented publications for the layperson

The Sierra Club*
101 Mills Tower
San Francisco, California 94104
  The *Sierra Club Bulletin;* legislation and action reference materials

Public Agencies—Federal

Council on Environmental Quality
722 Jackson Place NW
Washington, D.C. 20006
  Annual reports on national status of environmental issues

Environmental Protection Agency
Office of Public Affairs
Washington, D.C. 20460
  Free citizens' bulletin; catalog of environmental publications

National Science Foundation
Washington, D.C. 20554
  Funding and development of scientific research and science education programs

U.S. Department of Agriculture
Washington, D.C. 20013
  Forest service: education and information materials and assistance; Soil conservation service: county or district offices for materials and technical assistance

U.S. Department of the Interior
National Park Service
Washington, D.C. 20240
  Land management and interpretive materials; newsletter and classroom aids, such as *Johnny Horizon*

---

*Check to see if organization has affiliate in your state.

U.S. Government Printing Office
National Referral Center
Library of Congress
Washington, D.C. 20402
   Directory of Information Resources in the U.S., including physical
   sciences, biological sciences, social sciences, water, scientific, and
   technical information sources

Public Agencies—State

Department of Education
   Directory of environmental education services

Department of Public Affairs
   Directory of state agencies and officers to contact on environmental
   affairs

Planning Area or County Offices
   Regional environmental planning and programs; county extension and
   field stations

Public Agencies—Local

Conservation Commission or other
community environmental agency
   Directories of local environmentally related organizations

Town or City Hall
   List of local officials with environmental responsibilities

Appendix B

Environmental Education Sources

Bibliographies (A Selected List)

Anglemyer, Mary, Eleanor R. Seagraves, and Catherine C. LeMaistre. *A Search for Environmental Ethics. An Initial Bibliography.* Washington, D.C.: Smithsonian Institution Press, 1980.

Carvajal, Joan, and Martha Munzer. *Conservation Education—A Selected Bibliography.* Danville, Ill.: Interstate Press, 1968.
————. 1970. *Supplement.*

Education Associates. *Environmental Education Abstracts and Index from Research in Education, 1966–1972.* Worthington, Ohio, 1973.

Environmental Conservation Education. Danville, Ill.: Interstate Press, 1974.

Gale Research Co. *Environmental Education Information Sources.* Detroit, Michigan, 1975.

National Education Association. *Environmental Education: An Annotated Bibliography of Selected Materials and Services Available.* Washington, D.C., 1974.

U.S. Educational Resources Information Center (ERIC). This is a federal clearinghouse for all publicly funded projects, curriculum materials, bibliographies, and research work. ERIC Indices are found in most college libraries along with information on ordering publications.

Warren, Betty. *The Energy and Environment Bibliography. Access to Information.* rev. ed. San Francisco, Calif.: Friends of the Earth Foundation, 1978.

Activity Guides

Many activity guides are one-volume books with a number of different ungraded activities. Others are in the form of packets, cards, or pamphlets. This selected list includes guides that are excellent resources and worth looking for, though some are no longer in print.

Allman, A.S., and O.W. Kopp. *Environmental Education: Guideline Activities for Children and Youth*. Columbus, Ohio: Charles E. Merrill, 1976.

American Geological Institute. *Environmental Studies Packets*. Olympia, Wash.: Essentia, Evergreen State College. Six different packets, n.d.

Baker Science Packets. *Baker Nature Study Packet*. Holland, Michigan, 1961. Grades 1–9.

Busch, Phyllis. *Urban Discovery Manual. 75 Stimulating Ideas for Investigating Some Common Urban Resources*. Columbus, Ohio: ERIC/SMEAC, 1969.

Gross, Phyllis, and, Esther P. Railton. *Teaching Science in an Outdoor Environment*. Berkeley, Calif: University of California Press, 1972.

Hug, John W., and Phyllis J. Wilson. Curriculum Enrichment Outdoors. New York: Harper & Row, 1965. (Out-of-print but a good reference.)

Jorgensen, Eric, Trout Black, and Mary Hallesy. *Manure to Meadow to Milkshake*. Los Altos, Calif.: Hidden Villa, 1978.

Outdoor Biology Instructional Strategies (OBIS). Berkeley, Calif.: Lawrence Hall of Science, 1974–1979. (Four volumes.)

Project KARE. *A Curriculum Activities Guide to Interdisciplinary Environmental Studies*. U.S. Education Resources Information Center, ERIC Document ED 157 682, 1976.

Roth, Charles E., and Linda G. Lockwood. *Strategies and Activities for Using Local Communities as Environmental Education Sites*. Columbus, Ohio: ERIC/SMEAC, December 1979.

Russell, Helen Ross. *Ten-Minute Field Trips*. New York: Doubleday, 1970.

Schults, Beth, and Phyllis Marcuccio. *A Guide to Learning*. Columbus, Ohio: Charles E. Merrill, 1972. (Includes activities and skill cards.)

Stapp, William B., and Dorothy A. Cox, eds. *Environmental Education Activities Manual*. Farmington Hills, Mich., 1979. (Order from authors.)

Swan, Malcolm D., ed. *Tips and Tricks in Outdoor Education*. 2nd ed. Danville, Ill.: Interstate Press, 1978.

University of the State of New York. *Living Within our Means: Energy and Scarcity; Environmental Education Instructional Activities*. Albany, New York, n.d. (Two volumes.)

VanderSmissen, Betty, and Oswald Goering. *Leader's Guide to Nature-Oriented Activities*. 3rd ed. Ames, Ia.: Iowa State University, 1977.

Van Matre, Steve. *Acclimatization*. Martinsville, Ind.: American Camping Association, 1972.

———. 1974. *Acclimatizing*.

———. 1979. *Sunship Earth*.

Wheatley, John, H., and Herbert L. Coon. *One Hundred Teaching Activities in Environmental Education*. Columbus, Ohio: ERIC/SMEAC, 1974.

Curriculum Series

In recent years, major textbook publishers have included ecology units or an entire environmental series in their elementary and secondary textbook publications. For those unfamiliar with these publications, a selected list of specific units or series follows, with particular emphasis on grades K to 6. These publications are available in the curriculum libraries of teaching colleges and universities.

Addison-Wesley Publishing
Reading, Massachusetts 01867
  STEM Science Series. Grades K–6

Interstate Printers and Publishers
19-27 North Jackson Street
Danville, Illinois 61832
  SEE(Self-Earth Ethic). Grades K–12; life-centered curriculum

Harcourt Brace Jovanovich
757 3rd Avenue
New York, New York 10017
  The Social Sciences: Concepts and Values. Grades K–6; Emphasis on basic ecology concepts; separate materials for Junior High

Houghton Mifflin
2 Park Street
Boston, Massachusetts 02107
  Earth Science Curriculum Project. Upper grades; includes interdisciplinary textbook and pamphlets

  Man and His Environment. Junior High; life science investigations

Holt, Rinehart and Winston of Canada
55 Horner Avenue
Toronto, Ontario, Canada M8Z 4X6
  Examining Your Environment Series. Grades 7–9; with activity cards

McGraw-Hill
1221 Avenue of the Americas
New York, New York 10020
  Elementary Science Study (ESS)

Rand McNally
Box 7600
Chicago, Illinois 60680
  SCIS (Science Curriculum Improvement Study). Grades K–6; with teachers' guides

Silver Burdett
250 James Street
Morristown, New Jersey 07960
  Adventure in Environment. Grades 5–6; developed by National Park Service; units, instructions, activities, and picture packet

John Wiley & Sons
605 Third Avenue
New York, New York 10016
  Nuffield Foundation Series. Developed in Great Britain with United States distributors

Curriculum Materials by Organization

Biological Sciences Curriculum
Study
Post Office Box 930
Boulder, Colorado 80306
  Publishes biology series, including green version with ecology emphasis; journals and workshops for junior and senior high teachers

Conservation and Environmental
Studies Center
Whitesbog Road
Browns Mills, New Jersey 08015
  Science, math, and history units for Grades K–12, with interdisciplinary environmental education emphasis

ECOS Community Association
833 Fox Meadow Road
Yorktown Heights, New York
10598
  Grades K–12; curriculum guides and environmental education programs

Education Collaborative for Greater Boston
Project WALSE
319 Arlington Street
Watertown, Massachusetts 02172
  Units on water, air, land, and solar energy; community curriculum materials with urban emphasis

Education Development Center
55 Chapel Street
Newton, Massachusetts 02158
  Social studies, math, and science curriculum guides and materials for elementary and secondary levels

Educational Facilities Laboratories
477 Madison Avenue
New York, New York, 10022
  Materials on school sites, facilities, community resources

Environmental Science Center
5400 Glenwood Avenue
Golden Valley, Minnesota 55422
  Grades K–12; units and inexpensive curriculum materials on all aspects of environmental education; environmental discovery units

Institute of Environmental Education
8911 Euclid Avenue
Cleveland, Ohio 44106
  For Junior and Senior High School students; curriculum materials
  especially with problem-solving approaches

Massachusetts Audubon Society
Education Department
Curriculum Materials Center
Lincoln, Massachusetts 01773
  Educational materials for all ages listed in "Zero in on Environmental
  Education, Natural History and Environmental Affairs"; publication
  for children, *Curious Naturalist*

Minnesota Math and Science
Teaching Project
University of Minnesota
Minneapolis, Minnesota 55455
  Grades K–3; teaching units in the MINNEMAST series

National Association for Environ-
mental Education
Post Office Box 400
Troy, Ohio 45373
  Grades 4–8; curriculum guides in environmental studies; publishes
  The Environmental Communicator and *Current Issues in Environmen-
  tal Education*

National Audubon Society
Educational Services
950 Third Avenue
New York, New York 10022
  List of publications available on request, including aids for teachers

National Education Association
1201 16th Street, NW
Washington, D.C. 20036
  Task force studies and reports on environmental education

National Science Teachers Association
1742 Connecticut Avenue NW
Washington, D.C. 20009
  List of science programs and curriculum materials for environmental
  education and energy curriculum materials

National Wildlife Federation
Educational Services Center
1412 16th Street NW
Washington, D.C. 20036
  Environmental discovery units; *Ranger Rick* magazine for children,
  educational supplement for teachers; wildlife week materials for
  schools and communities

Purnell Library Services
Division of MacDonald–Raintree
205 West Highland Street
Milwaukee, Wisconsin 53203
  Interdisciplinary projects for elementary grades in outdoor environments

Rodale Press
Education Services Division
Emmaus, Pennsylvania 18049
  Grades 7–12; units on recycling, science with garbage, soils, foods, and compost; can be adapted for lower grades; also publishes environmental action bulletin

Scholastic Earth Corporation
Scholastic Magazine
Englewood Cliffs, New Jersey
07632
  Grades 1–6; multimedia units emphasizing awareness

University of Delaware
College of Education
Newark, Delaware 19711
  Grades K–12; published population curriculum study in 1971

Xerox Education Publications
Education Center
Columbus, Ohio 43216
  Grades K–12; ecology and pollution units

Appendix C

Reference Sources

Some of the sources cited in the references following each section of this manual are not readily available in bookstores and libraries and can best be obtained by writing to the organization that published the material. Included below are the names and addresses of these organizations, except for those already included in Appendix B.

American Camping Association
Bradford Woods
Martinsville, Indiana 46151

Antioch/New England Graduate School
Land Use Curriculum Project
Keene, New Hampshire 03431

Association for Childhood Education International
3615 Wisconsin Avenue, N.W.
Washington, D.C. 20016

Data Courier, Inc.
620 South Fifth Street
Louisville, Kentucky 40202

Dembar Educational Research Services, Inc.
Post Office Box 1605
Madison, Wisconsin 53701

Education Associates
Post Office Box 441
Worthington, Ohio 43085

Education Development Center
55 Chapel Street
Newton, Massachusetts 02158

Education Facilities Laboratories
477 Madison Avenue
New York, New York 10022

Enterprise for Education
10960 Wilshire Boulevard, Suite 2134
Los Angeles, California 90024

Environmental Science Center
5400 Glenwood Avenue
Golden Valley, Minnesota 55422

W.H. Freeman
660 Market Street
San Francisco, California 94104

Gale Research Company
Book Tower
Detroit, Michigan 48276

Garrard Publishing Company
1607 North Market Street
Champaign, Illinois 61820

Girl Scouts of the U.S.A.
830 Third Avenue
New York, New York 10022

Hawthorn Books, Inc.
260 Madison Avenue
New York, New York 10016

Heldref Publications
400 Albamerle Street NW, Suite 500
Washington, D.C. 20016 (*Journal of Environmental Education*)

The Home and School Institute
c/o Trinity College
Washington, D.C. 20017

Institute for Environmental Awareness
Post Office Box 821
Greenfield, Massachusetts 01302

Institute for Environmental Education
8911 Euclid Avenue
Cleveland, Ohio 44106

Iowa State University Press
South State Avenue
Ames, Iowa 50010

The Izaak Walton League of America
1800 North Kent Street, Suite 806
Arlington, Virginia 22209

Massachusetts Audubon Society
The Education Department
Curriculum Materials Center
Lincoln, Massachusetts 01773

National Geographic Society
17th and M Streets NW
Washington, D.C. 20036

Office of Conservation Education
The Resources Agency
Sacramento, California 95814

Pennant Press
8265 Commercial Street, No. 14
LaMesa, California 92041

Project Adventure
Post Office Box 157
Hamilton, Massachusetts 01936

Professional Educators Publications, Inc.
Box 80728
Lincoln, Nebraska 68501

Project KARE/E3
Montgomery County Intermediate Unit No. 23
Montgomery Avenue and Paper Mill Road
Erdenheim, Pennsylvania 19118

Regional Center for Educational Training
45 Lyme Road
Hanover, New Hampshire 03755

Sage Publications, Inc.
275 South Beverly Drive
Beverly Hills, California 90212

Stapp, William B., and Dorothy A. Cox
32493 Shady Ridge Drive
Farmington Hills, Michigan 48018

Stipes Publishing Company
10–12 Chester Street
Champaign, Illinois 61820

Teachers and Writers Collaborative
84 Fifth Avenue
New York, New York 10011

Thorne Ecological Institute
2336 Pearl
Boulder, Colorado 80302

University of California Press
2223 Fulton Street
Berkeley, California 94720

University of Minnesota Press
2037 University Avenue SE
Minneapolis, Minnesota 55455

Warwick Publishing
2616 NW 33rd
Oklahoma City, Oklahoma 73112

Western Publishing Company
850 Third Avenue
New York, New York 10022

Appendix D

Organizing an Environmental Education Training Course— Strategy and Procedures

ELBANOBSCOT MODEL

The training course model in this manual was used by Elbanobscot to train teachers, students, teacher aides (both volunteer and paid), community leaders, and youth group leaders, as well as individuals seeking enrichment. Therefore, the material presented can be adapted to meet a variety of needs.

To organize similar training courses general suggestions relating to the Elbanobscot model are outlined below. The rationale and procedures for each session are contained in the summary of the course in the Introduction.

Responsibilities

Determine what work needs to be done to organize the course and how the work will be divided. For example, who is responsible for preparation of course materials and information aids, for contacting session leaders, for determination of site location(s), for publicity, evaluation of homework, course content? Brief job descriptions and periodic meetings to review responsibilities will help the course run smoothly. Taking care of details can be as important to the overall success of the program as providing relevant topics and experiences.

At Elbanobscot the course coordinator oversaw the procedural aspects of preparing and running the course, with assistance from a volunteer librarian and staff public relations aide. The staff program director cooperated on determining course content and ran several of the workshops.

Costs

To determine the course cost for participants, calculate materials, overhead, staff and teacher salaries, and any other costs of running the course. Expenses can be kept to a minimum by mobilizing local environmental resource people as instructors on a volunteer basis.

Elbanobscot encouraged PTA's, schools, garden clubs, churches, and youth groups to sponsor participants.

Publicity

Provide descriptive information on the training course in plenty of time (3 to 5 weeks) to attract participants.

Elbanobscot publicity took the form of letters to members, news articles in local papers, and notices and personal presentations to schools and educational groups. Personal contact with likely candidates recommended by past participants and by educational groups proved most successful.

Locations

Hold sessions at more than one location to show how a variety of environments, including the most barren and/or altered, can lend themselves to environmental education learning experiences.

Materials

In addition to background and activity handouts, have books, periodicals, curriculum materials, audiovisuals, and other educational aids on display to show the richness of information and ideas available for the environmental trainee.

At Elbanobscot participants received a training course schedule including dates and locations of each session at the beginning of the course. Participants were asked to read some background materials in advance of each session. A library was available throughout the course, and nearby resource centers were recommended.

Session Leaders

Use a variety of teachers to provide different teaching approaches and different sources of expertise.

If the Elbanobscot course coordinator or program director was not actually involved in the subject coverage, at least one was on hand in a supervisory role for each session to encourage homework evaluation and group participation and interaction.

Number and Order of Sessions

The basic model calls for 10, 2-hour sessions (including two nature and ecology workshops). If you are giving teaching credit, more than 20 hours of course time may be needed. If you are undertaking youth group leadership training, you may need fewer sessions. If you are working with teachers of younger aged children, you may want more emphasis on the nature and ecology workshops, which can be developed for at least four sessions. For teachers of older children and adults, the stress may be more on environmental issues, and the material presented herein can be expanded upon with specific information on community issues and problem-solving approaches.

There is no required order of sessions. Much depends upon when you can get the right people to teach certain topics and seasonal opportunities. However, information on course goals and basic environmental education and ecology concepts are essential at the outset if other material is to have relevance. A progression of ideas and approaches should reinforce these concepts throughout the environmental education training.

Tone

Informality and friendliness are key ingredients in building a good learning atmosphere. Sharing and mutual support encourage the involvement and participation of all class members. The group should be learning from each other.

Avoid lecture approaches. Sit around a table indoors or in a circle in the field during background presentation and discussion time, and facilitate group interaction as well as personal discovery during field activities. The same environmental education approaches should be used during the course as are advocated for use by participants who will be teaching students after the course.

Attitudes

Encourage car pooling, recycling, sharing resources and information. By example and by reminder, leaders can make participants aware of each individual's role in protecting the environment.

Elbanobscot asked participants to bring coffee mugs to store at headquarters for use during the course. Participants brought in recycled items for class activities, such as chlorox plastic bottles and other containers. Information on environmental meetings, workshops, and legislation was shared by the group, and a bulletin board was kept up to date.

Course Requirements

Make clear the requirements of your course in terms of attendance, work, and evaluation procedures. Spell out details such as times, locations, and recommended dress for each session.

At Elbanobscot a certificate was issued if no more than two sessions were missed, and the participant was actively engaged in class programs and follow-up activities. Missed sessions were made up during the following course. Elbanobscot worked with nearby high schools and colleges to determine their requirements for students seeking credit.

Homework

Assignments should not be optional since they represent an important practical ingredient of the course, that is, experience in applying the skills and information gained in each session. However, vary the assignments according to the group. Participants may suggest an alternate assignment or work on a continuing project throughout the course. They may work alone, in a group, or with one partner, as desired. A brief period at the beginning of each session to review previous homework, concepts, and skills covered is helpful and encourages continuity.

Evaluation

Constantly evaluate the course and each participant's progress through discussions of homework and its practical application. The final evaluation takes place at the summary session.

Many changes in content and teaching took place as the Elbanobscot training course evolved because of the written and verbal comments of the participants during the summary session. For example, providing more practice teaching opportunities, going over homework assignments of the previous week at the beginning of each session, and planning special workshops were suggestions that were implemented. Since the backgrounds, interests, and aims of class members were varied, their evaluation responses also were varied. Quite often a weakness for one person was a strong point for another. Therefore, the course was not changed willy-nilly but as a result of a recurring request from several people. Evaluation also continually occurred among Elbanobscot staff to ensure that the course was responsive to the needs of a changing suburban population.

Follow-Up

As the participants begin using their training, provide additional support in the form of workshops, meetings and newsletters. They will also benefit from a communication network that allows them to share ideas and information with course leaders and other participants. You can use these follow-up programs to evaluate how effective their training has been and how it has been used. Keep in touch with institutions which use trained teachers or aides to receive comments on the value of the training and suggestions for improvement.

APPENDIX REFERENCES: (A)

ADULTS Institute for Environmental Education. *An Environmental Education Guide for Workshops*. Series C, Rev. Printing. Cleveland, Ohio, Jan. 1976.

McInnis, Noel, and Don Albrecht. *What Makes Education Environmental?* Louisville, Ky.: Data Courier and Environmental Educators, 1975.

National Education Association. *Guide to Planning and Conducting Environmental Area Workshops*. Washington, D.C., 1972.

State Departments of Education and State Universities, for information on workshops and training programs.

Index

Environmental (*cont.*)
  attitudes, 5, 40, 161–163, 166–170
  concepts, 9
  encounters, 157–158
  ethic, 5
  literacy, 5, 9
  programs, 153, 157–158
Environmental education, concepts, 47
  definitions, 3–4
  evaluation of, 46, 178
  integrating into curriculum, 46–47
  sources, 181–187
  teaching and learning, 36, 39–42, 178
Environmental Education Act, 3
Environmental issues, 5, 9, 21, 152–153,
      156–158, 164, 166
  activities, 154–155, 161–163, 166–171
    attitudes survey, 161–162
    community environmental profile, 154–
      155
    environmental auction, 161, 163
    home, school and community, 166–171
  identifying, 152–153, 156–157, 166
  problem solving, 156–159
Erosion, 60, 121
Evergreen (*see* Conifer)
Evaluation, of environmental education prog-
      rams, 46, 178
  of training course, 175–179, 193

F

Fall, 77, 115
  activities, 79, 82, 85
    animals, 79
    food gathering, 85
    tree change, 82
Field, 17, 24–25, 85
Field notes, 66, 82
  habitat activity, 22–23
Field trips
  activities
    creative writing, 63–64
    dig a trashpile, 66–69
    local cemetery, 61–62
    rock, 60–61
    rotting log, 62–63
    soil profile, 65–66
    vacant lot, 64–65

  planning procedures, 28, 57–59
  sites, 58–60
  teaching and learning, 58–59
Fish, classes of, 91
Food chains, 17–19, 21–24, 114, 138
Food pyramid, 17, 26
Food sources, 37, 82, 84–86, 166–167
Food webs, 17–18, 22, 24
Forest, 18, 73
  activities, 22, 25, 78–82
    animals, 78–79, 82
    camouflage, 25
    floor debris, 79, 82
    habitats, 22
    urban comparisons, 79–82
Frogs, 91–93, 111, 114
  tadpole activities, 116–117

G

Galls, 101
Games, 32, 136–137, 178
  animal classification, 24
  ecology, 23, 165
  food chains, 24
  habitats, 24
  interrelationships, 24
  invent a name, 146
  plants, 146
  predator/prey, 11
  role playing, 160, 164–165
  web of life, 24, 138
Geology, 60–61, 121–126

H

Habitat, 13, 19, 21, 32–33, 108, 113
  activities, 22–24, 64–65, 82, 96, 117
    bird, 96
    field notes, 22–23
    game, 24
    plant comparisons, 82
    urban, 64–65
    water, 117
  definition of, 16
History (*see* Social studies)
Human, environmental impact, 25, 64–65,
      82, 152–156

Massachusetts (*cont.*)
  Walden Pond, 123
Mathematics, 32
  archaeology use, 67–68
  metric system, 50
  temperature study, 119
  tree population activity, 24
Matter, 18
Metamorphosis, complete, 89
  incomplete, 89–90
Minerals, 24, 60
Microorganisms, 17–18, 24–25, 79
Music, 32, 48, 51, 64, 143–145

N

Native Americans, 69, 85, 137, 141
  activities, 142–143
    animal bones, 143
    cattails, 142
    clay, 142
    shells, 143
    stones, 143
Nature study, 4–5, 31
Nature trails, 29, 32–33, 178
  activities, 32, 34, 36–37
    developing, 34
    self-guiding booklet, 32, 36
  benefits of, 33
  curriculum enrichment, 36–37
  planning suggestions, 34
Neighborhood (*see* Community)

O

Organic, 24, 66, 169
Organisms, 16–19, 21–25, 62, 73, 79, 82,
    113, 116
Outdoor, 57
  behavior, 42, 178
  classroom, 32–33
  education, 4–5
  teaching, 28, 32, 40–42, 64, 178

P

People (*see* Human)
Photosynthesis, 17–18, 82–83

Physical environment, 16, 18, 22, 26, 121–
    125
  activities, 125–130, 167–170
    energy uses, 167–170
    geology studies, 125–126
    pollution in snow, 127
    preserving snowflakes, 127
    snow gauge, 126
    solar oven, 130
    solar studies, 129–130
    sun clock, 130
    windvane, 130
Piaget, Jean, 43, 45
Plant kingdom, 73–77
Plants, 19, 32, 73, 85
  activities, 24–25, 48–49, 61, 79, 83–86,
      100–102, 115–116, 118, 129, 137,
      139–140, 142, 146–147, 149, 167
    animals, 100, 102, 107
    aquarium building, 115–116
    brainstorming, 167
    cattails, 118, 142
    craft projects, 137, 139–140
    decomposing, 83, 102
    in forests, 79
    galls, 101
    non-flowering, 83
    populations, 24
    rocks, 61
    seeds, 25, 48–49, 146–147
    in soil, 24
    tree rings, 149
    wild foods, 84–86
    winter, 129
  classification of, 73–76
  historical uses, 37, 84–86
  identification of, 75–76
  interdependence of, 20, 22
  interrelationships, 22, 26, 64–65
  poisonous, 33, 84
  in water, 108, 111–115
Poetry (*see* Language arts)
Pollution, 18, 20–21, 154, 164
  activities, 124, 126–127, 164, 167,
      169
    school, 167, 169
    snow, 126–127
  attitudes toward, 164, 169
  causes of, 124, 167